Empowering Social Workers for Practice

WITH VULNERABLE OLDER ADULTS

Barbara A. Soniat
Monica Melady Micklos

NASW PRESS

National Association of Social Workers
Washington, DC

James J. Kelly, PhD, ACSW, LCSW, President
Elizabeth J. Clark, PhD, ACSW, MPH, Executive Director

Cheryl Y. Bradley, *Publisher*
Lisa M. O'Hearn, *Managing Editor*
John Cassels, *Project Manager*
Dac Nelson, *Copyeditor*
Lori J. Holtzinger, *Proofreader*
Tom Fish, *Indexer*

Cover by Blue House
Interior design by Xcel Graphic Services
Printed and bound by Victor Graphics

© 2010 by the NASW Press

Library of Congress Cataloging-in-Publication Data

Soniat, Barbara A.
Empowering social workers for practice with vulnerable older adults / by Barbara A. Soniat and Monica Melady Micklos.
    p. cm.
  ISBN 978-0-87101-395-8
  1. Social work with older people.   I. Micklos, Monica Melady. II. Title.
  HV1451.S643 2010
  362.6—dc22

                              2009053730

Printed in the United States of America

Contents

Acknowledgments

This book represents the results of over 15 years of university and practice community collaboration. We are particularly grateful for the decades of support provided through our affiliations with George Washington University Medical School, the District of Columbia Office on Aging, Iona Senior Services, Episcopal Senior Ministries (ESM), and the National Catholic School of Social Service of Washington, DC. More recently, we have been encouraged by the work of the American Bar Association's Commission on Law and Aging, which, in collaboration with the American Psychological Association, has produced capacity assessment guides for judges, lawyers, and psychologists. This book is presented in recognition of the valuable contributions that social workers have made throughout the history of the profession to assessing older adults within the context of their social environments and promoting the dignity, worth, and rights of vulnerable populations, including vulnerable older adults.

Many social workers, social work interns, and professional members of several interdisciplinary geriatric assessment teams have debated, modified, applied, and tested the concepts and the practice model articulated in this book. We are especially grateful to social workers and field educators Deborah Blum, Pat Larson, Christine Jackson, Karen Currie, Henriette Kellum, and Fiona Druy, who have used the capacity–risk model in their presentations, teaching, and practice. We thank Paul Huizinga for his role in incorporating concepts from our practice model into the statewide training curriculum for social workers in Virginia.

We extend special thanks to colleagues who reviewed and provided feedback on drafts of our manuscript: Richard Millstein, Jean Toomer, and Regina Bernard. We are especially grateful to Pat Micklos, who edited multiple versions of the document with a keen eye for detail and love of language that only a retired English teacher could provide. Special thanks to NASW Press and John Cassels, our project manager, for making this book a reality.

I (Barbara A. Soniat) am grateful to my husband, Bob Washington, for his encouragement, patience, and support throughout the process of creating this book and to my daughter and grandchildren—Sonia, Joey, Jazmine, and Jada—for their consistent faith and encouragement.

I (Monica Melady Micklos) would like to thank my husband Jeff, whose love and encouragement made the writing of this book possible, and our four children

Acknowledgments

Samantha, Zachary, Katherine, and Emily, whose excitement about Mom writing a book was energizing. Special thanks go to Mary Ann Buckley and all the care managers who have worked for ESM Cares for providing me the opportunity to guide them in a social work practice that has had such a powerful and positive effect on so many older adults in the Washington, DC, metro area.

About the Authors

Barbara A. Soniat, PhD, MSW, is an associate professor at the Catholic University of America's National Catholic School of Social Service (NCSSS) and director of its Center on Global Aging. She teaches MSW practice courses and a course on clinical social work practice with older adults, and she is co-principal investigator for a Council on Social Work Education gero-ed project. Dr. Soniat also serves as a commissioner for the American Bar Association's Commission on Law and Aging. She has worked in the fields of social work and gerontology for over 30 years. For over 20 years, her career effectively integrated clinical practice, research, teaching, and interdisciplinary field-based education of professional students. Dr. Soniat is the former long-time director of the George Washington University (GWU) and IONA Senior Services geriatric assessment and case management programs, where for over two decades she implemented collaborative partnerships between a university medical center (GWU), a public agency (the Washington, DC, Office on Aging), a private agency (IONA Senior Services), and several schools of social work (NCSSS, Howard University, University of Maryland, Virginia Commonwealth University, University of Pennsylvania, and University of Alabama) and departments of psychiatry (GWU and Georgetown University). Through these endeavors, she has worked with many social workers, case managers, student learners, and colleagues to develop, test, modify, and refine models and tools for education, research, and practice with vulnerable older adults. Dr. Soniat has a strong interest in pursuing answers to practice-generated research questions. She is a featured speaker at national, international, regional, and local conferences.

Monica Melady Micklos, MSW, was the founding director of ESM Cares, a geriatric assessment and care management service under the auspices of Episcopal Senior Ministries of Washington, DC. For the past 18 years, she has worked with various institutions that are committed to promoting best practices and increasing the competencies of social workers who practice with vulnerable older adults. In her continuing efforts to improve quality of life for older adults, Ms. Micklos is currently developing a professional service that provides training and supervision to social workers and senior service agencies. She is coauthor of a model for assessing capacity of older adults and has presented workshops discussing concepts of the model at numerous local, regional, and national conferences. Ms. Micklos's MSW is from the Catholic University of America's National Catholic School of Social Service. She has also held social work positions at Georgetown University Hospital and Prince George's County Hospital.

Introduction

Social workers are frequently the first responders in situations that require assessment of an older person's ability for independent decision making and self-care. Social workers in a variety of practice settings have to make decisions about when to refer cases for adult protective services (APS), crisis mental health interventions, or legal services; these decisions often involve assessing functional capacity and risks. Social workers in senior centers and senior volunteer programs are sometimes called on to discharge older persons when they experience diminished capacity to continue to participate in senior programs or exhibit inappropriate, inconsistent, or unsafe behaviors because of changes in functional capacity. Social workers also work in settings that provide opportunities for early identification of older persons who may be developing problems managing their care in the community. There is limited professional literature to inform and guide social work practice in the area of assessing capacity and working with vulnerable and at-risk older adults. Other disciplines also recognize the need for professional guidance in working with those persons who have diminished capacity. In 2005, the American Bar Association (ABA), in partnership with the American Psychological Association (APA), published *Assessment of Older Adults with Diminished Capacity: A Handbook for Lawyers*. This extremely timely document was the culmination of 10 years of collaboration between the ABA and APA. Subsequent products that were derived from the collaboration include a handbook for judges on determining capacity (ABA, APA, & National College of Probate Judges, 2006) and a handbook for psychologists on assessing capacity (ABA & APA, 2008).

This text provides guidance for social workers who are assessing capacity and making intervention decisions involving older adults with diminished capacity. Part One provides background information about social work practice with vulnerable older adults. Chapter 1 presents the demographic challenges that make it imperative that geriatric social workers are empowered with knowledge and skilled for community-based practice with the elderly. We describe the population of vulnerable older adults who are likely to require ethically guided, culturally sensitive assessment of their capacity to exercise their rights to self-determination. We also summarize concepts related to assessing capacity used in the medical, psychiatric, and legal arenas and recognize the reality that evaluating capacity (or "competence") goes beyond the legal arena. Chapter 2 discusses geriatric social work with a particular emphasis on community-based practice. This chapter emphasizes the need to empower geriatric social workers to recognize their own expertise and the important role they play with the growing population of vulnerable older adults. We also identify the assessment of capacity as an emerging area of practice within the field of social work and promote the social work "person-in-environment" perspective as well suited to offer a valuable contribution toward improving the quality of capacity assessments. Chapter 3 discusses the value issues and ethical dilemmas that surface in work with this population. Chapter 4 covers the theoretical basis for the capacity–risk model.

Part Two, chapters 5 through 8, discusses use of the capacity–risk model for assessing vulnerable older adults. This includes a chapter on the importance of establishing a therapeutic alliance with the older adult, chapters applying the biopsychosocial framework to the assessment of capacity and risk, and a chapter on assessing the ability of the individual to function in his or her environment using the capacity–risk model. Part Two ends with illustrations of how social workers can use the capacity–risk model to guide decisions about interventions with vulnerable older adults.

Part Three uses cases to demonstrate the capacity–risk model in working with specific populations of vulnerable older adults, such as older adults with compulsive hoarding behaviors, and those who neglect their self-care needs.

Social workers who practice in geriatric, mental health, and APS settings play critical roles in assessing functional capacity and risks encountered by vulnerable older adults living in homes and communities. This population includes older persons at various stages of dementia (some of whom have become disengaged from the healthcare system), older persons with chronic mental illnesses and those who are without family and informal support networks. In hospital settings, social workers routinely carry out some level of evaluation of their patients' capacity when they work with them on discharge plans. At times, this evaluation identifies older patients who need guardians appointed to make healthcare decisions, legal interventions to facilitate placement in nursing homes when they lack close kin, or conservators to protect their finances, property, and assets. Community-based social workers often are involved in working with attorneys to implement interventions for their older clients that provide "less restrictive alternatives" to court interventions. Geriatric social workers often collaborate with physicians, psychiatrists, psychologists, and attorneys throughout the process of addressing the needs of vulnerable older adults, including those with diminished capacity.

Both of us have served as directors of community-based geriatric assessment and case management programs. We have observed that social workers were often frustrated by their efforts to work with older clients who needed assistance but refused to accept help. In these situations, the social worker often grapples with difficult ethical and legal issues concerning when to intervene against a person's will and when to respect his or her right to self-determination. In the early 1990s, we collaborated with professional case managers and graduate social work interns to develop the capacity–risk model, a conceptual guide for assessment and interventions with vulnerable older adults who live in high-risk situations, but resist accepting help (Soniat & Micklos, 1996). We have used the capacity–risk model in educational, training, consultation, and supervision sessions with professional social workers and social work students. The capacity–risk model also has been used in interdisciplinary training and consultations with physicians, psychiatrists, nurses, and attorneys. The presentation of the capacity–risk model at the 1993 Southern Gerontological Society Annual Meeting (Soniat & Micklos, 1993) resulted in requests for consultations, in-service trainings, and follow-up presentations at local, regional, and national conferences such as conference workshop presentations for: the District of Columbia Office on Aging (Soniat & Micklos, 1994), the American Society on Aging (Soniat & Micklos, 1995a), the Maryland Gerontological Society (Soniat & Micklos, 1995b), the Network of Episcopal Professionals Providing Aging Services (Soniat & Micklos, 1998), the NASW DC Metro Chapter (Soniat & Micklos, 2007), and ESM Cares and Sunrise Assisted Living (Soniat & Micklos, 2008). Over the past 15 years, it has become an integral part of the statewide training program for APS workers in Virginia; part of the content of the two-day course titled "Assessing Capacity" is based on the capacity–risk model (Virginia State Board of Social Services, 2001).

This book addresses the gap in knowledge about the role of social workers in assessing and treating the problems of vulnerable older adults. The text discusses skills effective for working with this population and presents the capacity–risk model to guide social workers with assessment and intervention decisions. The use of the capacity–risk model can help social workers generate evidence to support client self-determination and guide recommendations for sustaining older adults in community settings when appropriate. Use of the model can also, conversely, generate evidence that guides social workers toward protective interventions and alternative placements when these are more appropriate for a particular situation. This text also provides information to strengthen the knowledge base and skills of the general population of social workers whose practice involves assessing and intervening with vulnerable older adults. Demographic trends and the expanding demand for highly skilled geriatric social work practitioners to work with increasingly complex situations encountered by vulnerable older adults living in communities across the country and globally support the need for this text.

PART ONE

PART ONE

CHAPTER 1

Vulnerable Older Adults: A Population Demanding Attention

IMPACT OF DEMOGRAPHICS ON SOCIAL WORK PRACTICE

The population in the United States and most other countries in the world is aging dramatically. In 2007, individuals over age 65 composed 12.6 percent of the population in the United States. By the year 2030, projections indicate that 72.1 million Americans will be over age 65 (see Figure 1) and that older adults then will make up nearly 20 percent of the U.S. population (U.S. Department of Health and Human Services [DHHS], Administration on Aging, 2008). Especially significant is the fact that projections show that the greatest increase will be among the oldest and most vulnerable subgroup of seniors, those over 85 years of age (DHHS, Administration on Aging, 2008; Hooyman & Kiyak, 2005). In 2000, adults over 85 years of age accounted for approximately 12 percent of the total senior population (Americans over age 65); by 2050, projections indicate that adults over age 85 will account for approximately 21 percent of Americans over age 65 (DHHS, Administration on Aging, 2008).

These demographic trends are increasing the demand for highly skilled geriatric social work practitioners to work with older adults living in communities across the country. The Institute for Geriatric Social Work (IGSW) estimated that 28 percent of social workers work primarily with older adults (IGSW, 2005). In the NASW survey *Assuring the Sufficiency of a Frontline Workforce*, 75 percent of the social workers who responded reported having older adults in their caseloads (Whitaker, Weismiller, & Clark, 2006). The number of social workers working with seniors will only increase as the percentage of seniors in this country booms.

Although the demand for social workers trained in geriatrics is growing, the number of social workers attending graduate MSW programs that offer an aging concentration or expanded courses on geriatrics is minimal. In its 2004 report

Figure 1: Numbers of People in the United States Age 65 and Older, 1900–2030

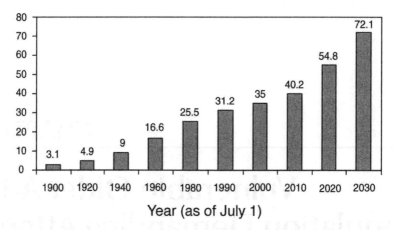

Year (as of July 1)

Notes: Adapted from Figure 1 (p. 3) in U.S. Department of Health and Human Services, Administration on Aging (2008). The *y*-axis represents numbers in millions.

An Aging Infusion: Gerontology Finds its Place in the Social Work Curriculum, the John A. Hartford Foundation reported that less than 3 percent of master's degree students were enrolled in gerontology programs in 2000; less than 10 percent of faculty members in 117 master's programs had formal training in aging; one-fourth of the 117 accredited master's programs lacked a single gerontology course; and two-thirds lacked even one field supervisor who was an expert in aging. As a result, social work graduates often lack the competencies they need to understand the complex requirements of older adults. A gap exists between the demands on the social work profession to work with older adults and their families and the preparation of the social work workforce to do so (CSWE, n.d.).

A growing concern in the field of gerontology is the steep rise in prevalence rates of functional incapacity among older adults, particularly those over the age of 85 (Wiener, Hanley, Clark, & Van Nostrand, 1990). The physical health of older people typically declines with increasing age while the likelihood of having a dementia escalates with age. In 2001, 24 million people worldwide had Alzheimer's disease and the expectation is that this number will rise to 43 million by 2025, and to 81 million by 2050 (Ferri et al., 2005). Adults age 85 and older are more likely to have a cognitive impairment and other coexisting health issues impairing their function (Wan, Sengupta, Velkoff, & DeBarros, 2005). A recent study found that limitations on activities of daily living increase with age, with the highest rate of limitations on activities of daily living occurring among people 85 and older (see Figure 2).

The majority of seniors who need long-term care are taken care of at home, with informal unpaid family care accounting for about 80 percent of caregiving activity (Kelly, 2008). The parent support ratio (the ratio of the population age 85 or over to that of ages 50 to 64) indicates that the level of support that families may be able to provide to their oldest members is decreasing worldwide. By 2050, people who are themselves well past middle age will be three times more likely than they are today to be responsible for the care of older relatives (United Nations,

Figure 2: Percentages of People with Limitations in Activities of Daily Living (ADLs), by Age Group: 2006

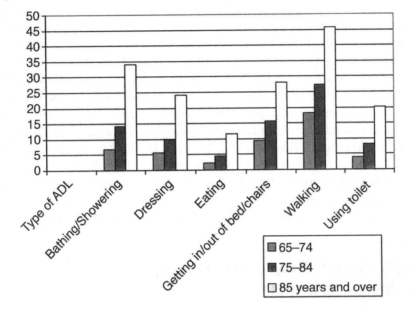

Notes: Adapted from Figure 9 (p. 14) in U.S. Department of Health and Human Services, Administration on Aging (2008). The *y*-axis represents percentages.

2007). Put otherwise, adults 85 years of age and older have the highest rate of limitations in their activities of daily living and are the fastest growing portion of the population, yet the level of support families may be able to provide (the parent support ratio) is projected to decrease. Given these trends, we anticipate more and more social workers and other healthcare professionals in the United States and throughout the world will find themselves working with vulnerable older adults.

VULNERABLE OLDER ADULTS

Vulnerable older adults are defined as seniors with limited cognitive or physical ability who are at risk for harm or neglect and seniors with impaired cognitive or physical ability who lack adequate support from family or an informal support network (Rothman, 1994). Vulnerable older people may present with a variety of problems. Examples include older individuals who are self-neglecting, hoarding, or socially isolated; those who suffer from mental illness or multiple coexisting health impairments; and elderly individuals who are facing eviction, homelessness, or other crisis situations. At times, social workers face challenging situations when the vulnerable older adult they are prepared to assist does not want help and refuses offered intervention and services. This can leave a social worker feeling frustrated, professionally inadequate and with great concern for the well-being of the older adult. Social workers often experience internal and external pressure to "do something" from their own value system, the referral source, or others in the older adult's network.

Feeling frustration that one will have to "wait for the next crisis" before intervening is common.

Most professional codes of ethics include language that requires respect for clients' rights to self-determination. The legal, psychiatric, and medical professions have grappled with the difficult task of defining the scope, circumstances, and situations in which this right can be overridden (Moye, Butz, Marson, Wood, & the ABA–APA Assessment of Older Adults Working Group, 2007; Zarit & Zarit, 2007). In contrast, adult protective service (APS) workers, geriatric social workers, geriatric care managers, home care professionals, public health nurses, and other clinicians have limited guidelines for addressing similar situations they encounter in community-based practice (Davis, 1992, McCue, 1997). These professionals attempt to rely on both the legal concept of competence and the medical doctrine of informed consent. Although relevant, these concepts do not fully address the unique issues that confront professionals who attempt to work with "at-risk" clients who do not agree to accept help and who are still in the community setting.

PERSPECTIVES ON EVALUATING CAPACITY: SUMMARY BY DISCIPLINE

Medical or Informed Consent

Within health care, the medical literature relies on the concept of "informed consent" to ensure that its practitioners respect patients' rights to choose or refuse medical care. The doctrine of informed consent requires that the patient is provided sufficient information to make an informed decision; the patient makes the decision voluntarily, free from undue influence or duress; and the patient has decision-making capacity (Altman, Parmelee, & Smyer, 1992). The Uniform Health-Care Decisions Act defines *decision-making capacity* to give medical consent (or "consent capacity") as "an individual's ability to understand significant benefits, risks, and alternatives to proposed health care and to make and communicate a health-care decision" (National Conference of Commissioners on Uniform State Laws, 1993). An evaluation of decisional capacity generally considers the patient's ability to communicate a choice, ability to understand the relevant information, ability to appreciate the medical consequences of the situation, and ability to reason about treatment choices (Appelbaum, 2007). A risk–benefit ratio developed for conceptualizing medical decisions suggests that the degree of competence or level of capacity needed to give informed consent for treatment varies on the basis of degree of risk and benefit of the treatment (Appelbaum, 2007; Appelbaum & Grisso, 1988).

During the past 30 years, a substantial body of case law has focused on the issue of informed consent and surrogate decision making associated with medical practice. This literature, however, is not always relevant to community-based practice with "at-risk" clients. Most often, medical decisions involve consent for clearly defined procedures and short-term treatment interventions. Furthermore, the fact that the client has the cognitive capacity to give informed consent (consent capacity) does not address the question of whether or not the client has the functional capacity to live independently. In community-based practice with "at-risk" older clients, the issues are often less well defined and recommended interventions tend to be long term.

Psychology and Neuropsychology

Cognitive impairments in older adults can be caused by distorted thought processes caused by psychiatric problems (such as psychosis or severe depression) or they can be caused by deficits to neuropsychological functions in attention, short- and long-term memory, judgment, problem solving abilities, insight, expression of information, orientation to person, place and time, and other areas of cognition relevant to decision making (Zarit & Zarit, 2007). Various mental status exams are often used to evaluate the older adult's cognition. Psychological and neuropsychological evaluations of an older adult's cognitive ability are often sought in capacity evaluations. Neuropsychological tests can help clarify the causes of the cognitive impairment and then evaluate if any of the causes can be treated to decrease the cognitive impairment (American Bar Association [ABA] & American Psychological Association [APA], 2005; Zarit & Zarit, 2007). Psychological and neuropsychological assessments can also help differentiate between dementia and depression, identify if the client's cognitive impairment is a result of brain damage, and can attempt to identify the cause of the brain damage, such as Parkinson's disease, Alzheimer's disease, stroke, or long-term abuse of alcohol. Identifying the presence of a treatable dementia or determining the cause for brain damage helps clarify the older adult's prognosis and intervention options.

Although useful for clarifying potential causes of cognitive impairment and important for ruling out reversible causes of cognitive impairment, the effectiveness of psychological and neuropsychological exams in evaluating older adults' capacity to carry out certain activities (such as those necessary for continuing to live in their own homes) varies. Auditory and visual deficits can influence the older adult's ability to communicate and respond adequately to questions in a structured interview. Level of education can also positively or negatively affect scores. For example, mental status tests do not necessarily identify dementia in well-educated people who can score in normal ranges despite developing obvious deficits in other areas of function (Zarit & Zarit, 2007). Michael McCue (1997) discussed the relationship between neuropsychological testing and an individual's function. Although there is a relationship between an individual's scores on neurological tests and his or her ability to carry out activities of daily living, McCue stated these findings were not strong enough to support definitive predictions about any given individual's capacity to care for self, to perform specific instrumental tasks, or to predict how the individual might function in response to specific demands such as balancing a checkbook, paying rent, or operating a piece of equipment. This is because of, in part, the fact that neurological evaluations, psychiatric evaluations, and neuropsychological testing are often measures of disease and disability, not the individual's functioning (McCue, 1997).

In 2007, the ABA and APA developed an assessment template for clinicians carrying out capacity evaluations for adult guardianship hearings (Moye, Butz, et al., 2007). It includes areas of assessment that are broader than the traditional psychological and neuropsychological assessments and incorporates functional elements such as evaluating abilities to complete common activities of daily living. This is a positive development and a valuable contribution to the field of capacity assessment in working with vulnerable older adults.

The current text adds to the growing body of knowledge in the field of capacity assessment through its focus on capacity and functional assessment of older adults within the context of their social environment. This perspective is based on the "person-in-environment" (PIE) construct, the hallmark of social work assessment and intervention. The added dimension of "environmental context" requires social workers to also assess the "risks" inherent in the environment in which the older person lives. It is the combination of impaired capacity and environmental risks that informs social work assessment and intervention decisions.

Legal

"Capacity" refers to the assessment of ability in specific areas. A clinician who conducts an assessment of capacity for the court would comment on the person's abilities, whereas a judge would decide on competence. "Competence" and "incompetence" are legal terms decided by a judge who has weighed all the evidence in a guardianship hearing. Guardianship is a legal proceeding undertaken to give a person or agency rights over another person who has diminished abilities to manage some or all of his or her personal or financial affairs (Mayhew, 2005). Although the particulars regarding how guardianship is dealt with differ from state to state according to state laws, the essential goal of the guardianship hearing is for the court to determine if the subject is incapacitated and whether a substitute decision maker needs to be appointed to act in an individual's best interest. When a person is determined to be incapacitated, the court considers if the guardianship would solve the issue (provide for the essential needs of the individual) and confirm there are no other feasible, less restrictive alternatives (ABA & APA, 2005; Mayhew, 2005). When these conditions are met, the court assigns a guardian as a substitute decision maker to act in the subject's best interests. Guardianship orders can be global or limited to the specific realms in which the person has been found to lack capacity (Zarit & Zarit, 2007).

Although the notion of what incapacitated means varies, most state laws have relied on some or all of the following three concepts: (1) the presence of a disabling condition; (2) level of functional behavior (ability to provide for personal needs); and (3) an evaluation of cognitive abilities or decisional capacity (Mayhew, 2005). The 1997 Uniform Guardianship and Protective Proceedings Act (UGPPA) offers the states a new framework for guardianship. The UGPPA provides a definition that removes the disabling condition and states that an "incapacitated person" is "an individual who is unable to receive and evaluate information or make or communicate decisions to such an extent that the individual lacks the ability to meet essential requirements for physical health, safety, or self-care, even with appropriate technological assistance" (UGPPA, 1997). Although the framework and definitions provided have helped the movement toward national standards, each state can still decide independently if it wants to enact the UGPPA in its entirety, consider parts of it, or use none of it. The variation regarding individual state laws is further complicated by each state's interpretation of the language within the UGPPA that assesses incapacity in light of "appropriate technological assistance" as requiring a "necessity element" before a person will be judged incapacitated (Mayhew, 2005).

Zarit and Zarit (2007) summarized the legal statutes regarding competence as typically addressing four key points on capacity. First, capacity is presumed until a court decides otherwise. Second, capacity is evaluated for specific abilities. A person can be found to lack decision-making capacity for a single ability but could be considered capable of carrying out all other activities. Third, legal definitions of incapacity usually include four components: (1) presence of a disabling condition; (2) cognitive impairment; (3) functional impairment; and (4) the need for another party to intervene to prevent harm or other adverse consequences to the individual. And fourth, incapacity involves more than just eccentricity or engaging in risky behavior.

Over the last couple of decades, most states have modified protective laws to consider capacity rather than "competence" and implemented provisions for surrogate decision making of incapacitated adults by family members, powers of attorney, and other advance directive tools, without the need for court intervention. This has enabled family members and other appropriate surrogate decision makers to authorize needed care without having to go through a tedious and costly court process. This is effective in situations in which the impaired senior either agrees with the planned interventions, or in situations in which he or she is unable to communicate any disagreement. When a senior with impaired capacity disagrees with concerned family members or other involved professionals who are seeking to set up a surrogate decision maker, or when a senior with impaired capacity decides to terminate the authority of the surrogate decision makers already put in place, court proceedings to determine competency become necessary to override the senior's wishes and implement a care plan against his or her will.

There is a growing recognition of the conflicting complex issues involved in guardianship determinations for seniors who want to continue living in their homes but who are considered at risk and are resistant to accepting help. To reduce subjectivity, many states refined the threshold for incapacity determinations by changing from broad language considering one's "ability to take care of oneself" to more focused language regarding one's "ability to take care of the essential requirements for one's physical health or safety" (Sabatino, 1996, p. 11). The two standards that have developed and are now included in some state measures for evaluating capacity to remain at home are "essential needs," which is sometimes called "endangerment," and "least restrictive environment." "Essential needs" refers to whether a person is able to provide for his or her own basic requirements, such as food and housing, or whether his or her efforts to do so are so poor as to cause endangerment. The legal standard of living in the "least restrictive environment" recognizes that there are advantages to remaining at home that can offset risk, particularly if remaining at home is what the person wants and if he or she understands the risks involved. The implication of this standard is that risks associated with remaining at home need to be balanced against the benefits and risks associated with moving to a protected setting. The goal of least restrictive environment frequently conflicts with the preferences of some families, guardians, and judges to avoid any possible risk of harm to an older person (Zarit & Zarit, 2007).

EVALUATING CAPACITY AND "COMPETENCE": NOT JUST A LEGAL ISSUE

The presumption that evaluating when to intervene against someone's wishes (their capacity or "competence") is only a legal issue for the courts to decide is inaccurate. By tradition, the term "competence" referred to legal judgments and the term "capacity" referred to clinical determinations. This distinction, however, is not consistently reflected in either legal or medical usage (Appelbaum, 2007). Although situations requiring guardianship are resolved in a court of law, often the initial assessment on capacity and intervention decisions regarding whether or not to override the older adults' right to refuse help occurs before the legal system ever gets involved. In fact, it is probable that the majority of determinations of diminished capacity in older adults are made by clinicians, APS workers, social workers, and other professionals outside of the legal arena (Moye & Marson, 2007). For example, when social workers request temporary medical commitment of their clients, refer their clients to a legal agency requesting petition for appointment of a guardian, or coordinate their older clients' discharge from the hospital to a nursing home on the family's authority, the social workers have based these intervention decisions on their assessment of the older clients' capacity.

Many of the interventions social workers recommend for their vulnerable older clients are based on their own professional evaluation of their client's capacity. Because social workers are frequently on the front lines, they are often one of the professionals conducting assessments of vulnerable older adults living in the community, determining which cases to refer for emergency services and which cases to bring to the attention of attorneys and the court system for consideration of a surrogate decision maker. Each time the social worker implements a plan based on the wishes of the client, the social worker has made the decision that the client has the capacity to understand and is competent. In general, it is only when the social worker feels the client lacks the capacity that the process of formally evaluating capacity and considering protective interventions is considered.

Community social workers must often grapple with questions such as which community agency, if any, has the responsibility for responding to concerns about older clients who are at risk and refuse help. Social workers who work with vulnerable older adults should understand APS laws, the guardianship process, what is required of professionals in their state, and what limits or constraints are present on professional interventions with clients who resist accepting help. APS laws vary from state to state. Most state APS laws must balance the state's duty to protect its impaired citizens with civil rights of the individual citizen. Many situations fall outside the purview of APS laws. In addition to APS laws, some communities have separate guardianship laws, mental health laws, and other legal interventions. However, these laws rarely address the preliminary assessments and interventions that must occur before one determines that a particular legal intervention is appropriate, warranted, and in the best interest of the client.

Legal doctrine is based on a presumption of capacity, that adults are free to make their own decisions, including the decision to refuse medical and social services, unless they have been judged and determined incompetent by a court (ABA, APA, & National College of Probate Judges, 2006; Smyer, Schaie, & Kapp, 1996; Wolff, 1990). This creates a catch-22 situation for community social workers working with resistant older clients, as one may have to go through a long process of interventions prior to presenting a case for surrogate decision making, or, if necessary, a legal competency hearing. Strict adherence to legal guidelines (and social work values of self-determination) might suggest that no intervention with clients who are refusing the assistance, including assessment, can legitimately be undertaken prior to a court's involvement. A well-respected legal authority on capacity assessment in the elderly raised the issue of examining "the policy of whether professionals ought to be encouraging or discouraging extralegal 'bumbling through' handling of persons with questionable capacity rather than routinely initiating formal judicial involvement through the guardianship process" (Kapp, 2003, p. 83). This perspective highlights the need for social workers to more clearly articulate their role and professional competencies in working with vulnerable older adults. The social worker's determination of when it is appropriate to "initiate formal judicial involvement" is anything but "routine" or a process of "bumbling through."

The social worker's comprehensive assessment of vulnerable older adults' capacity and function is vital in clinical, family, community practice, and the judicial process. Social workers provide information on family structures, family functioning, and the quality of family relationships that is critical when considering issues related to surrogate decision making. In geriatric community-based practices, many potential guardianship cases do not result in guardianship petitions because social workers work with attorneys and other professionals to implement interventions that provide "less restrictive alternatives" to court interventions. These alternative interventions attempt to strike a balance between their clients' coping ability and their environmental demands, and usually seek to ensure clients' safety and protection, while maximizing clients' autonomy, independence, and involvement in decision making.

SUMMARY

The changing demographics of our aging society will result in a need for education and training of more social workers to work effectively with the older population. Vulnerable older adults who are at risk and resistant to accepting help present especially challenging dilemmas for community professionals. Resolving the issues raised by these situations requires careful consideration of individual and professional value systems and mastery of professional skills for working with this population.

We have traditionally looked to the fields of law, medicine, psychology, and neuropsychology to guide us on assessment of cognition and decisional capacity. Although relevant, they do not fully address the issues present when evaluating capacity in older adults within the context of their environment. There is a need for more tools and models based on social work concepts to guide practice with vulnerable older adults.

CHAPTER 2

Geriatric Social Work as a Vital Field

Geriatric social workers contribute to improving the quality of services to older adults by applying social work knowledge, values, and skills to working with vulnerable older adults who have diminished capacity for independent decision making. This chapter provides an overview of geriatric social work practice and highlights the value of the social work person-in-environment (PIE) perspective for the assessment of functional capacity of vulnerable older adults. The authors advocate broader recognition of social work as one of the mental health professions that plays a significant role in evaluating and supporting older adults with impaired functional capacity, their families, and informal support networks. Social work practitioners who focus on mental health and case-management practice with older adults require specialized skills that enable them to determine when individuals and families need supportive interventions that may include adult protective services (APS) or court petitions for guardianship.

GERIATRIC SOCIAL WORK PRACTICE: OVERVIEW

Geriatric social workers assist seniors and their families in multiple settings and on a wide array of issues ranging from medical and mental health, housing, transportation, home care, legal, financial, and more. Geriatric social workers provide guidance, support, and services that help to improve and maintain their client's quality of life. The advocacy and oversight geriatric social workers provide can reassure seniors and their families that they are receiving the best healthcare, home care, and senior housing services possible. Whitaker, Weismiller, and Clark (2006) stated that geriatric social workers help older clients and their families to negotiate healthcare and social welfare systems, to provide resources essential to living and to address the challenges that come with aging. Brian Hofland, director of the aging program at the Atlantic Philanthropies, described social workers whose practice involves older adults with complex care needs as "often the linchpins helping individuals and their families coordinate and navigate a care plan involving multiple providers and support systems" (Whitaker et al., 2006).

Geriatric social workers work with older adults in a variety of settings. In community-based settings, there is great demand for geriatric social workers to work with older adults in areas such as case management services and adult day care programs. Healthcare settings (such as medical centers, outpatient clinics, hospitals, nursing homes, rehabilitation centers, hospices, or assisted living communities) rely on social workers to assist their "patients" or "residents," the majority of whom are older adults. In 2005, NASW outlined standards for social work practice in healthcare settings (which includes geriatric social work practice) to include assessment, care, and interventions that "address the physical, mental, emotional, and social well-being of the person; and address prevention, detection, and treatment of physical and mental disorders with the goal of enhancing the person's biopsychosocial and spiritual well-being" (p. 12). The expertise of geriatric social workers is also needed in many of the mental health settings, including inpatient psychiatric hospitals, group homes for the mentally ill, substance abuse programs, family or group therapy programs, and individual psychotherapy services. Even within the administrative or macro settings, more social workers are finding themselves dealing directly or indirectly with geriatrics, such as running a retirement community or helping community planners evaluate and plan for the needs of an aging United States. There is a growing number of "age-in-place" communities that benefit from the guidance of geriatric social workers, who help them evaluate their current and future needs and consider options for structuring support services, funding issues, long-term care insurance options, and other community system needs. As this country examines the best way to meet its aging society's needs to maintain quality of life and to manage costs, an understanding of community systems, or the macro perspective, is a growing and vital area of geriatric social work.

Although the role of social workers is influenced by the settings in which they practice and the organizations for which they work, competent practice requires social workers to have a solid knowledge base of aging and mental health and to use strong clinical, case management, and advocacy skills in their practice. Many geriatric social workers in case management with older adults provide comprehensive biopsychosocial assessments of their clients, evaluate their ability to function within their home environment, and, if appropriate, coordinate support services that enable their clients to continue living in their own homes (Yagoda, 2004). If remaining home is not possible or desired, geriatric social workers can identify new living arrangements, assisted living, or other retirement communities that provide the appropriate level of care and that maintain lifestyle and other quality-of-life indicators.

The goal of geriatric social work practice is to assist older people "to maintain independence; optimize physical, psychological, and social functioning, including contribution to the community; and maximize the quality of life" (CSWE, 2009). The geriatric social worker working with vulnerable older adults in the community provides a comprehensive assessment that includes gathering information on the client's physical health, orientation, memory, mental health, ability to perform activities of daily living, support network, economic resources, home or living environments, and the risks present. The environmental context is an important factor affecting the geriatric social worker's assessment of the client's ability to function. Understanding the interaction between the client and his or her environment enables the social worker to recommend interventions that seek to strike a balance between the client's coping ability and the client's environmental demands (Compton & Galaway, 1989). Functional assessments are important in geriatric social work practice. Functional assessments identify the individual's strengths and weaknesses, as well as obstacles in their environment that affect effective functioning. By using a functional assessment framework, social workers focus on what the older person is actually doing or not doing in particular situations, under certain conditions, and in light of their unique demands in their environment (McCue, 1997).

Clinical skills are critical, as carrying out mental health assessments and providing support and counseling to the client and family members through periods of stress, transition, and illness is often part of the geriatric social worker's role. Geriatric social workers often need to evaluate their older clients for mental health issues such as depression, dementia, and suicide risk. Some of the common issues older clients present with include having difficulty coping with the death of their spouse, adjusting to retirement, changes in their abilities and daily routine, coping with chronic illness, experiencing acute illness and hospitalization, and dealing with a move to a rehabilitation or nursing facility.

Some geriatric social workers also work with older clients who may have major psychiatric diagnoses such as paranoid schizophrenia, obsessive compulsive disorder, anxiety disorder, antisocial personality, or other mental health issues. The community-based geriatric social worker may be the first mental health provider to come into contact with an older adult who has had a change in physical health and who needs assistance (such as home care), but whose psychiatric issues create a barrier to receiving that care. Although some of these clients may be known to the mental health system their entire lives, others may never have been diagnosed. These situations require the geriatric social worker to use strong clinical skills to evaluate the client's mental health needs, to evaluate the safety of the client and others, and to use relationship-building and other clinical skills to reduce the client's anxiety and increase his or her willingness to receive additional mental health and other services.

Strong communication skills are essential as the geriatric social worker often serves as a liaison with family members and other care providers such as medical, financial, legal, and spiritual advisors. The geriatric social worker needs the skills to clearly present his or her assessment, provide recommendations, and facilitate discussion among involved parties. Mediation skills, which help to bring consensus regarding a plan of care, are important for the geriatric social worker, as well as having the skills to effectively implement and monitor the client's care plan. The geriatric social worker needs to know about the various services in the community to identify appropriate resources, such as medical and mental health care services, home care services, senior housing, transportation services, day care programs, entitlement programs like Medicaid and Supplemental Security Income, nutritional programs, legal assistance, money management assistance, pharmacy assistance programs, assisted living, nursing home placement, or APS.

VALUING THE SOCIAL WORK PERSPECTIVE FOR ASSESSING CAPACITY

Much of the literature on assessing capacity in older adults is geared toward medical, psychiatric, and legal assessments. In these assessments, the term "capacity" primarily refers to the individual's physical and mental abilities. The field of social work offers a perspective in which the assessment considers the interaction between clients (with their physical and mental abilities) and their environment. The clients' environment includes information such as the homes in which they live, their families, their support networks, and the values and risks present. Grisso (1986) argued that the "environmental context" (the external situations to which the older adult must respond) is critical in defining which specific functional abilities are most salient when evaluating capacity in older adults, especially related to legal competency judgments. Because different contexts require different functional abilities, the question is whether the individual has the level of functional ability to cope effectively in a particular environmental context (Lawton, 1982; Willis, 1996).

Few texts specifically approach capacity assessment from a social work or PIE perspective. One exception is a 1997 report by Kane and King that examined assessment of capacity in environments that included case management and community care programs, hospital discharge planning, and APS. Another exception is Greene, Cohen, Galambos, and Kropf (2007), who discussed geriatric social workers' use of Lawton's (1982) environmental press model to assess the competence of their older adult clients to remain living in their homes. This viewpoint considers "competence" from the PIE perspective and highlights the concept of goodness of fit (which refers to having an appropriately supportive environment). The 2007 text by Greene and colleagues is a valuable contribution to social work literature on working with older adults. It recognizes competence as fluid and affected by the environment, which encourages the social worker to work with the older adult on interventions that improve functional capacity.

The current text adds to the growing body of knowledge by including a framework for evaluating the vulnerable older adult's psychosocial function, which incorporates indicators from the client's biopsychosocial and risk assessments and considers the interaction between the client capacity and risk. This conceptual model, the capacity–risk model (developed by the authors), considers how the older adult's level of capacity and level of risk act together, and provides social workers guidance for interpreting their assessment information and making intervention decisions in their work with vulnerable older adults with impaired capacity. The capacity–risk model identifies the level of function clients may need to continue to make their own decisions given their situation and environment. It enables the social worker to offer a perspective that is based on the social work PIE construct and that is effective for decision making regarding what level of involuntary interventions may be appropriate in situations when the older adult is at risk and resistant to accepting services. The capacity–risk model offers the aging community, legal community, and other professionals working with this population a valuable and unique viewpoint to capacity assessment and intervention decisions.

RECOGNIZING OUR EXPERTISE

It is important to recognize the broad roles and expertise of geriatric social workers and to promote the value of including the social work perspective when evaluating capacity in vulnerable older adults. Because social workers function in diverse settings with varied responsibilities, the role of social workers as geriatric mental health providers may not be as familiar a role as are some of the other specialized areas of social work practice. Even within the social work profession, the knowledge, skills, and roles of geriatric social workers may not be widely recognized, and they often are undervalued. For example, the *Social Work Dictionary* defines "case management" as "a procedure to plan, seek, and monitor services from different social agencies and staff on behalf of a client" (Barker, 2003, p. 58). In reality, case management practice with vulnerable older adults (who tend to have multifaceted needs and greater risks) requires much more than simply linking clients with resources. Prior to identifying appropriate resources, the social worker must use strong clinical skills to carry out a comprehensive assessment, which then guides the development of the plan of care and eventually leads to the linkage of resources (Yagoda, 2004).

In a 2006 handbook for judges who are involved in determining guardianship cases, the American Bar Association (ABA), American Psychological Association (APA), and National College of Probate Judges provided a list of clinical professionals who may bring expertise to the capacity evaluation process, with descriptions intended to highlight their knowledge. The summary provided on the expertise of social workers states that "social workers are trained to consider the multiple determinants on an individual's social functioning and are often knowledgeable about a wide range of social and community services that may assist the individual" (ABA et al., 2006, p. 45). Although generally accurate, this description is also very limited and does not reflect the clinical skills used by many social workers. This description of social work and the definition of social work case management are examples that show the need to educate the broader field of social work, as well as other professionals, regarding the clinical skills of many geriatric social workers who are experienced in multiple areas of practice.

Social workers working as geriatric case (or care) managers are often clinicians who routinely carry out comprehensive biopsychosocial assessments and who work with their older clients, their clients' support network, and a diverse group of professionals to implement at times complex care plans. These care plans may include interventions that seek to provide the client with necessary support while maintaining as much independence for the client as possible. Working with older adults usually requires the social worker to develop proficiency in multiple practice areas that may overlap traditional divisions of social work. This is because of a number of factors. Many older adults have coexisting issues that could require simultaneous assessment and intervention from more than one practice area of social work. Also, vulnerable older clients seem to respond more positively when working through a therapeutic relationship that they have developed with one primary social worker who can provide continuity through multiple settings and situations. This is particularly true when the older client has some level of impaired capacity and is ambivalent, fearful, or resistant to accepting services (Soniat & Micklos, 1993).

For example, an 85-year-old woman whom we call "Mrs. Brown" is referred to a geriatric assessment and case management program by her children, who are concerned about her ability to continue living at home alone. The geriatric social worker assigned to Mrs. Brown carries out a biopsychosical assessment, meeting with Mrs. Brown in her home weekly. Mrs. Brown is a widow, having lost her husband a year earlier. During this past year, her children have noticed their mother's personal care and the condition of the house declining. Several utilities were turned off for nonpayment and stacks of mail remain unopened on the table. The social worker's assessment will include evaluating and gathering information from the client, her doctors, her family, and others regarding her health, nutrition, medications, recent changes, and evaluating her functional status including activities of daily living. The social worker will also seek information on Mrs. Brown's past history regarding her mental health, evaluate her for depression, memory loss, and screen for signs of potential cognitive impairment. The social worker will gather information about her deceased husband, children, family, friends, and support network, and seek to understand their level of involvement and support. The social worker also evaluates Mrs. Brown's resources, the home and neighborhood of Mrs. Brown, and risks present.

The social worker will spend time with Mrs. Brown to try to develop a relationship with her, obtain a sense from Mrs. Brown herself regarding how she is doing, how the loss of her husband has affected her, her daily routine, the areas she herself feels she needs assistance in, and her preferences for the future. Some of the meetings between the social worker and Mrs. Brown are spent with the social worker primarily providing supportive counseling to Mrs. Brown, who is feeling overwhelmed and alone. However, Mrs. Brown refuses a referral to see a therapist for depression or counseling. She, like many others in her generation, perceives an official mental health diagnosis as negative and will not consider going to formal counseling. She does appreciate and feel support from the social worker's weekly "sessions," and she views their talks as a helpful way for her to express her feelings about the loss of her husband, the changes in her life, and the difficulties she is having managing herself and her home.

The social worker analyzes the information she has gathered in her assessment and presents her assessment to Mrs. Brown and her children. The social worker reviews areas of concern such as Mrs. Brown's inability to carry out certain activities of daily living, memory loss, and other areas that affect her health, quality of life, and ability to continue managing at home independently. The social worker will make recommendations for areas that need further evaluation, such as psychiatric evaluation and consideration of antidepressive medication, and discuss how treatment for depression may decrease the memory loss and increase Mrs. Brown's ability to manage at home. The social worker also reviews options for increasing the amount of support in the home as well as other residential settings such as assisted living. Discussions regarding Mrs. Brown's personality, values, and lifestyle are taken into account.

While implementation of support services is in process, Mrs. Brown has a stroke and is taken to the hospital. During this time, the social worker sees Mrs. Brown while she is in the hospital, provides the hospital staff important information regarding Mrs. Brown's capacity prior to the stroke, and works closely with the hospital to identify a short-term rehabilitation center that would best fit her needs and personality. She recovers well and goes to a short-term rehabilitation program. The social worker continues to see Mrs. Brown at the rehabilitation center, providing supportive counseling and mediating some conflict with various issues Mrs. Brown is having at the facility. Mrs. Brown knows the social worker well and the relationship allows the social worker to address sensitive issues. The social worker works closely with the rehabilitation staff to encourage Mrs. Brown to accept an appropriate and needed amount of home care to enable her to return home and assists with obtaining documentation that enables her to qualify for sliding-scale subsidies, resulting in her being able to afford more home care assistance.

Like those of many vulnerable older clients, Mrs. Brown's needs require the geriatric social worker to wear many hats. This social worker is working in a traditional case management role, providing home visits and meeting with the client to evaluate her needs and risks within her home setting. She is also evaluating the client's mental health and providing supportive counseling. The social worker is working with this client, her doctors, and physical therapists on her home care or discharge needs as she moves through various parts of the healthcare system, from home to hospital to rehabilitation center and back home. Because the therapeutic relationship is so crucial for effective work with vulnerable older clients, more geriatric social work practitioners are seeking settings that allow them to practice with this generalist perspective. Empowering social workers to recognize and publicize their own expertise and encouraging them to be involved in the emerging practice areas for geriatric social work is essential for promoting growth in this critical area of practice.

CHALLENGES TO OBTAINING QUALITY CAPACITY ASSESSMENTS

The majority of capacity assessments occur outside of judicial review among family members, clinicians, attorneys, and staff in medical facilities (Moye & Marson, 2007). Standards physicians use to base their capacity judgments vary, with very low reliability and agreement between physicians who are evaluating capacity in patients with dementia (Marson, Earnst, Jamil, Bartolucci, & Harrell, 2000; Marson, McInturff, Hawkins, Bartolucci, & Harrell, 1997; Moye, Karel, Azar, & Gurrera, 2004; Moye & Marson, 2007). Although efforts are underway to improve the reliability of general clinical examinations, there are currently no established and validated criteria for capacity assessment in community-based settings (Moye & Marson, 2007). There is also a growing recognition that the quality of the capacity evaluations in the judicial setting needs improvement (ABA & APA, 2008; Moye & Marson, 2007). A study regarding the clinical information used by the court to determine guardianship showed great variability between states and even within states (Moye, Wood, et al., 2007). To assist clinicians who conduct capacity examinations, an assessment template was developed that identifies important areas of information for the clinicians to include in their assessment report for the court (Moye, Wood, et al., 2007). This template is a positive and important step to help standardize and improve the quality of the clinical evaluations submitted to the court for a petition of guardianship.

Although the development of a standardized instrument would greatly improve the consistency of the information required for assessment of an older adult's capacity, there are often practical challenges to obtaining the information. Having a physical exam and other medical tests are important for obtaining the information on the older adult's physical and mental health and for addressing active issues that could be impairing the older adult's health and functioning. In some cases, medical assessments from multiple disciplines (such as internists, geriatricians, and psychiatrists) may be needed. Oncologists, cardiologists, neurologists, and other specialists may also need to be consulted to clarify diagnosis, treatment, and prognosis information as it relates to the client's function. The number of disciplines and professionals involved, with various and sometimes overlapping roles, and without clear communication or coordination, can be a barrier to the older adult's ability to receive an effective comprehensive clinical assessment. In addition, coordinating these appointments among the older adult, his or her family, and the medical providers can be complicated. This is even more difficult when the vulnerable older adult does not want the medical and mental health evaluations that are recommended, refuses to see any of the doctors, and is generally resistant to accepting help. In these situations, traditional attempts to obtain evaluations often fail and, as a result, decisions regarding the older adult's capacity, and ultimately his or her competence, are made with incomplete clinical assessment information.

CAPACITY ASSESSMENT: AN EMERGING AREA OF PRACTICE

Because the fastest growing portion of the population is adults of age 85 and older, a group who have the highest rate of impairments in their activities of daily living, and because the percentage of available family caregivers (parent support ratio) is decreasing, we anticipate that many more social workers will come into contact with older adults who have some level of impairment and who do not have adequate support. A growing number of these vulnerable older adults are likely to become subjects of capacity evaluations in medical settings and in the judicial arena when a petition for appointment of a guardian for the older adult is being considered. One potential result will be an increasing demand for social workers trained in geriatrics to provide capacity assessments of their vulnerable older clients.

Recent studies highlighting concerns regarding the quality of clinical evaluations used in guardianship hearings have ignited a debate regarding what type of professional should be involved to achieve a clear picture of the capacity of the older adult who is the subject of the hearing. Although a majority of states (36) identify the physician as the primary clinician providing the clinical information, 23 state statutes allow the court to use a "mental health professional" either in lieu of a physician or to supplement the physician's evaluation and eight states require a multidisciplinary evaluation that combines a team of physicians, social workers, psychologists, nurses, or others (Mayhew, 2005). We believe that incorporating the social workers' PIE perspective, and their unique skills in effectively working with vulnerable older adults, improves the quality of the capacity assessment and of the intervention decisions. In addition, we promote the social work profession as one of the qualified mental health professions appropriate to conduct a capacity evaluation, independently or as a vital member of a multidisciplinary team, and seek recognition of the expertise of social workers in this role and their inclusion in state statutes addressing guardianship and protective proceedings.

Whether advocating for the older client who may be the subject of a capacity assessment or working at the macro level advocating for individual rights, protections and quality services for older people, more social workers need to become involved in the multidisciplinary effort to improve the quality and consistency of capacity assessments of vulnerable older adults in all arenas. Involving social workers in the capacity assessment can help improve the information gathered (Melady, 1992). Effective coordination and communication with various medical, psychiatric, and other professionals, both clinic and community based, is instrumental to the achievement of an accurate and quality assessment of the vulnerable older adult's capacity and function. This is even more important, and more challenging, when there are multiple professionals with various disciplines, located in different offices, agencies, or medical centers. In addition, engaging, involving, and communicating effectively with the older client who is receiving the capacity assessment and his or her family is critical. Among the areas that make the field of social work an effective discipline to provide this service are experience in case management and coordination of care, skills in working with older adults who may be resistant to receiving medical evaluations, the ability to effectively communicate within and between multidisciplinary teams, and a long history of working with individuals through home visits and within the context of their environment.

NEEDED: MORE SOCIAL WORKERS TRAINED IN GERIATRICS

Geriatric social work is the fasting growing practice area within the field of social work ("Geriatric Social Work," n.d.). Among geriatric social workers, capacity assessment of vulnerable older adults is one of the emerging and growing areas of practice. Although the need for social workers educated and skilled to work with older adults is increasing, the numbers of social work students exposed to courses in gerontology or gaining field experience in aging placements is not meeting the demand (Whitaker et al., 2006). With the expected boom in the aging population, this gap between the demands on the social work profession to work with older adults and the preparation of the social work workforce is likely to grow. Greater efforts are needed to increase the number of skilled geriatric social workers available to serve this country's needs, today and in the future. Steps to achieve this include expanding opportunities for social work students to enroll in courses with aging content and encouraging social work students and social workers already in the field to focus their career on aging.

The John A. Hartford Foundation has shown commitment to improving the care and well-being of older adults and their families today and for the future. Because the Hartford Foundation values the important role social workers serve in maintaining and improving the quality of life for older adults, it has developed a number of programs to strengthen geriatric social work education and prepare more aging-competent social workers in the field, such as the National Center for Gerontological Social Work Education (http://www.gero-edcenter.org). To facilitate the development of a larger workforce of competent geriatric social workers, the Hartford Foundation has offered grants to schools of social work for the purpose of infusing aging content into the core social work curriculum and supporting the establishment of competency-based geriatric social work education. A recent publication titled *Transforming Social Work Education: The First Decade of the Hartford Geriatric Social Work Initiative* (Hooyman, 2009) documented the impact the Hartford Foundation has already had on gerontological social work education. The gap between the demand for geriatric social workers and their availability could be further reduced if aging content were required for social work licensure and certification examinations and as part of the continuing education units necessary for renewal. This would likely increase the number of social workers exposed to gerontology and encourage highly skilled geriatric social workers to consider expanding their career or practice to offer education and training to their peers.

GERIATRIC SOCIAL WORK COMPETENCIES

In addition to helping to increase the number of students entering schools of social work to focus in the field of aging, and increasing the availability of aging courses and content, the Hartford Foundation has been working collaboratively to establish core competencies for geriatric social work. Competencies are measurable practice behaviors composed of knowledge, values, and skills; the goal is to demonstrate the social worker's successful integration and application of the competencies in his or her practice with individuals, families, groups, organizations, and communities (CSWE, 2009).

Establishing competencies for geriatric social work helps to ensure that social work practitioners in the field have the appropriate training and skills necessary to effectively serve the needs of older adults. Through the Hartford Foundation's funding and partnerships with the CSWE, the Center for Aging Policy Evidence Database and Public Policy Clearing House, the Social Work Leadership Institute, the New York Academy of Medicine Practicum Partnership Program, and Strengthening Aging and Gerontological Education in Social Work, a number of programs and tools have been developed, including the Hartford Practicum Partnership Program Scale for Geriatric Social Work, the Hartford Geriatric Social Work Initiative, and the national CSWE Gero-Ed Center (Greene et al., 2007).

These collaborative efforts helped to develop the CSWE Gero-Ed Center Foundation Gerontological Social Work Competencies. The Gerontological Social Work Competencies focus on gaining knowledge in four areas: (1) values, ethics, and theoretical perspectives; (2) assessment; (3) intervention; and (4) aging services, programs, and policies. To help assess student and social worker competencies, the Hartford Practicum Partnership Program and the CSWE Gero-Ed Center adopted a measurement tool called the Hartford Practicum Partnership Program Geriatric Social Work Competency Scale II. The skills identified in this tool include the ability to conduct a comprehensive biopsychosocial evaluation, ascertain health status and physical functioning (activities of daily living), evaluate cognitive function and mental health status, administer and interpret standardized assessment and diagnostic tools, and effectively use intervention skills. These intervention skills include areas such as ability to establish rapport, mediate situations with angry or hostile older adults and family members, provide case management services, advocate on behalf of older clients with agencies and other professionals, implement educational strategies to provide information to the older adults and their family on wellness and disease management, and more (CSWE, 2009). In addition to the assessment itself, the strength of the geriatric social worker's clinical skills is further evaluated in areas such as ability to enhance the coping capacities and mental health of older clients through a variety of therapy modalities, ability to use group therapy interventions, and ability to assist caregivers to reduce their stress and maintain their own physical and mental health.

SUMMARY

The demand for social work practitioners specializing in geriatrics is growing dramatically. Working with vulnerable older adults often requires the social worker to use skills in multiple practice areas. Encouraging students of social work to enter aging concentrations and promoting geriatrics as a vital field of practice is essential to meet the future needs of our aging county. There is also a need for social workers to play a central role working with vulnerable older adults to improve the process of capacity assessments, increase the consistency of information considered and improve the quality of the determination regarding the client's function and related intervention decisions. Social workers who master the geriatric social work competencies will possess the knowledge, skills, and perspective necessary to conduct clinical assessments, including evaluations needed by court systems for assessment of capacity and function in guardianship cases. Expanding competencies of social workers to evaluate capacity of vulnerable older adults and developing tools to guide assessment and intervention decisions is vital not only for geriatric social workers, but also for our society.

CHAPTER 3

Theoretical Perspectives

T he pursuit of social justice is a core social work value. It is critical that social workers who practice with older adults understand and recognize their role in promoting positive change in how society perceives and treats older adults, particularly those who are disadvantaged and vulnerable. Older adults have historically been a marginalized population. However, as a result of positive changes in longevity, health, education, active life styles, and civic involvement, more positive images and opportunities are emerging for older adults. As we experience these positive changes, it is very important that social workers remain cognizant of their role in promoting the interests and well-being of that segment of the older population that remains marginalized. This includes those who are poor, very old, or socially isolated and those with physical, mental, or functional disabilities.

EMPOWERED PRACTICE

Geriatric social workers often practice in interdisciplinary settings. Other professionals in those settings may not be aware of the values, knowledge, unique skills, holistic perspective, and capabilities that social workers bring to interdisciplinary practice settings. Social workers must practice from an "empowered" stance to engage in practices that empower their clients. The concept of "empowerment" as a framework for social work practice was first introduced by Barbara Solomon (1976) in the mid-1970s. Empowerment is an intentional, ongoing process involving mutual respect, participation, engagement, and appropriate sharing of responsibilities, decision making, power, and resources. Social workers bring critical and unique skills to geriatric practice through the profession's values, its person-in-environment (PIE) focus, and its accumulated knowledge base, derived from working with older adults across practice settings. Many interdisciplinary practice settings employ only one social worker. In these instances, social workers must assume professional leadership roles and assume responsibility for demonstrating the value that social work adds to the process of delivering services to older adults. When social workers rely on other members of the team to define their role, gaps can develop between the social worker's skills and capabilities and the expectations of other team members. To realize their potential for competent practice with older adults, social workers must commit themselves to continuing education and learning, critical reflection and evaluation of their practice, and keeping abreast of new evidence for practice generated by research.

It is also important for geriatric social workers to realize that there are areas of practice with older adults in which there is limited research to guide their practice. Extreme longevity, survival with multiple chronic illnesses, and the potential for long periods of life after significant peers have died are relatively new phenomena. Despite the lack of "evidence" for some interventions, professional decisions can have profound effects on the lives of older people, determining outcomes such as access to resources and services, discharge plans, and living arrangements. Responsible practice requires that geriatric social workers raise critical practice questions and engage in dialogue with professional peers, social work educators, and researchers to inform the education and research agendas for social work practice with older adults. Often, practice issues that are seen on the front lines of practice are hidden from social work gerontology scholars, sometimes because they affect relatively small numbers of older adults and don't show up in traditional surveys. For example, we know relatively little about older adults who experience problems with homelessness. They are a small part of the homeless population; only by deliberate sampling would they be included in research studies. Yet, from a practice perspective, they may be the most vulnerable and complex category of people who are homeless. Effective interventions with relatively rare populations require creative and innovative approaches, informed by existing knowledge, but also having the potential to contribute to the knowledge bases for social work practice. Social workers who are overburdened by excessive caseloads, staff shortages, paperwork, and limited support may not be effective advocates for their clients (Smith, 2008). Geriatric social workers need to be proactive to ensure that the values, preferences, and voices of older clients are heard, especially in fast-paced practice settings, such as emergency rooms and hospitals. Their clinical and advocacy roles are critical to ensure optimal services and care for vulnerable older adults.

There is a gap between research and practice, which means that social workers may not be aware of or informed about current findings from gerontological and social work studies (Ray, Bernard, & Phillips, 2009). There is a need for more collaboration among practitioners, educators, and researchers. A Canadian study estimated that only two percent of social work research is translated into practice (Macdonald, 2002); we do not have a corresponding estimate for the translation of research to practice in the United States. To effectively conceptualize research questions that address the situations that social workers encounter in practice, there is a need for greater collaboration among practitioners, academicians, and researchers. The capacity–risk model is one example of a conceptual model that was developed in response to questions generated by social workers from their practice with vulnerable older adult. The specific questions addressed by the model are these: Under what circumstances is it appropriate to override an older adult's right to self-determination? How do social workers assess for safety and "danger to self or others" in nonemergency, chronic situations involving older adults? Who decides what types and levels of risks are acceptable risks for older adults?

EARLY GERIATRIC SOCIAL WORK RESEARCH

The conceptual roots for the capacity–risk model were derived from reflections on research conducted in the late 1960s by social work pioneer Margaret Blenkner. As the first director of research for the Benjamin Rose Institute in Cleveland, Ohio, Blenkner led two landmark studies that used classical, randomized experimental design to evaluate the outcomes of social work interventions with older adults who were living in their own homes. Counterintuitively, initial results showed lower mortality rates for the control group—those who did not receive social work interventions. Further analyses of the data showed a correlation between social work interventions and nursing home placements. Blenkner's work showed that frail older adults who received social work services were more likely to be relocated to institutional settings; there was an association between change in living arrangements and increased mortality. "Her findings about services to the elderly often were contradictory to established wisdom and agency practice" (NASW, 2004). Blenkner developed the concept of "transfer trauma" to describe potential stress and risks associated with removing frail older adults from the familiarity of their home environments. Her work suggested that frail older adults may not have the physical, psychological, and social capacities to adjust to new environments, thus resulting in the decline in functional capacity that is sometimes observed with transitions from home to nursing home. The concept of "transfer trauma" focused attention on the potential risks involved in relocating frail older adults from familiar environments into apparently safer institutional care settings. Blenkner's work was controversial and at odds with accepted policies and practices in the emerging field of social work practice with older adults. Nevertheless, her work has influenced geriatric social work values and policies such as respecting clients' rights to self-determination, exploring alternatives to institutional care for clients who prefer to remain at home, incorporating interventions to reduce the impact of residential change and only implementing involuntary interventions as a last resort. The formulation of the capacity–risk model was an effort to incorporate these values and practice principles.

Subsequent studies, in other social science disciplines, have consistently reported a relationship between declining functional and cognitive abilities and change in living arrangements (Lichtenberg, MacNeill, & Mast, 2000; Worobey & Angel, 1990); yet Blenkner and social work research contributions to this knowledge base are rarely cited. Blenkner's research provided early support for policies and programs that made home health services available to sustain older people in their own homes. Her work also provided early evidence of the benefits of evaluative and applied research for improving social work practice with older adults.

ENVIRONMENTAL PRESS AND ECOLOGICAL THEORY OF AGING

M. Powell Lawton, a social psychologist, gained national recognition in the early 1960s for his pioneering work linking outcomes for older people with environmental factors. He identified the concept of "environmental press" and is credited with developing "the ecological theory of aging" (Lawton & Nahemow, 1973). Lawton and Nahemow's (1973) "adaptation model" suggests that people with higher levels of competence can adapt to a wider range of environmental press and have a greater chance of experiencing favorable adaptive outcomes than those with lower levels of competence. Lawton's research treats environment as a complex variable with both physical and social attributes.

> Environmental press is a [theory] of adaptation that focuses on personal variables (competencies), environmental variables (environmental press) and the interaction between the two. Competencies include physical and functional health, cognitive and affective functioning, and quality of life. Environmental press variables include the person's home environment, their social environment, and their neighborhood environment. The fit between the person's level of competencies and the demands from their environment affect how well the individual is functioning. (Lichtenberg et al., 2000, p. 54)

The ecological theory of aging has been used to study how living environment affects physical activity, which in turn affects health status (Shipp & Branch, 1999). The adaptation model and the ecological theory of aging continue to inform research and development in the architectural design of assisted living facilities, continuous care communities, and nursing homes. Occupational therapy researchers have used the ecological theory of aging to assess the fit between the older person and their physical home environment, and to examine the role of physical and social environments in every day competence and problem solving in older adults. The concept of environment press suggests that older adults do best when they have opportunities to engage and participate in social networks and social environments to the maximum of their abilities. Conversely, they lose abilities and skills over time, when constricted to environments that offer little or no "press" or demands; overly demanding environments can lead to stress, frustration, and loss of motivation (Nelson-Becker, Chapin, & Fast, 2009, p. 163).

Although the PIE construct is a historical cornerstone of social work theory and practice, direct and conscious application of the ecological perspective to social practice with older adults is relatively new (Nelson-Becker et al., 2009). The ecological perspective emphasizes individual interventions that are directed to promoting personal competence; the focus of environmental concerns is strengthening or establishing social supports (Greene, 1999). Social work practice from the ecological perspective seeks to achieve goodness of fit between person and environment. Strengthening the fit between people and their environments provides social work with a core function (Germain & Gitterman, 1986, p. 631).

The capacity–risk model is used to observe how an individual functions within his or her social environment. The concept of "capacity" parallels the concept of "competency" in the environmental-press framework; however, it is a broader measure that incorporates a biopsychosocial perspective (Engel, 1978). Later chapters elaborate how the capacity–risk model is used as a guide for assessing an older adult's capacity to function in their living environment, and how the functional capacity is used to guide professional decisions about an individual's ability to understand and make an informed decision about tolerable risks.

THE STRENGTHS PERSPECTIVE

Social work practice from a strengths perspective is a philosophy and approach to practice that moves from focusing on problems to looking at the strengths and potential that are embedded in every situation (Saleebey, 2008). This perspective is consistent with the changing presentation of aging in our society, as more people are living longer, healthier, active lives. However, even in practice with vulnerable older adults, social workers can accomplish more with and on behalf of their clients when they adopt the strengths perspective. It means a major shift from looking at deficits to becoming aware of the assets, opportunities, and potentials embedded in all human experiences.

The strengths perspective in geriatric practice represents a humanistic approach to social work interventions that can yield creative and innovative results. For example, adult protective service and geriatric social workers are often involved with older adults who need legal protective interventions like appointment of a guardian. Community social workers often view these situations as negative outcomes that result in taking away basic human and civil rights, especially when adults become "wards of the state" and a legal or public guardian is appointed. Once a guardian is appointed, social work services are usually terminated. However, humanistic practice, from a strengths perspective, has resulted in several new and innovative programs and roles for social work practice with older adults who have been adjudicated and deemed "incapacitated."

Geriatric case managers are sometimes hired by legal guardians to work collaboratively with them to assess and provide interventions that address the psychosocial needs of the person. In some jurisdictions, social workers are appointed as guardians, when the court evaluation process shows that the person's needs are more psychosocial than legal. A third example involves guardianship monitoring projects, in which courts provide funding for social work field education units. Graduate social work students, supervised by a social work educator, gain valuable clinical experience conducting annual psychosocial assessments of "wards of the court," to monitor the quality of guardianship services and to identify unmet needs. In these programs, social work students and their field instructor are empowered to report to the court on the psychosocial needs of an extremely vulnerable population, and to make recommendations to the court on their behalf. These examples show that when social workers are "empowered" they can empower older people who may be frail and unable to make their own decisions. When social workers function from a strengths perspective, they may be able to identify human needs that social workers are uniquely qualified to address.

The six key principles of the strengths perspective are these (Nelson-Becker et al., 2009):

1. All individuals have strengths at every stage of life and under all conditions.
2. All experiences, even negative or unexpected ones, may present opportunities for growth.
3. Traditional diagnosis and assessment in direct practice often make assumptions that limit rather than expand capacity.
4. Collaboration with an older adult client can motivate him or her to achieve his or her aspirations. Older adults may have important aspirations yet to accomplish.
5. Any environment has resources to be uncovered or co-constructed.
6. A civil society engages in care for all its members.

The capacity–risk model can be used by social workers as a tool to conceptualize use of the strengths perspective in work with vulnerable older adults. Using the capacity–risk model, social workers evaluate capacity along three dimensions: physical, psychological, and social. This holistic assessment of capacity results in a nominal measure (low, moderate, or high) of capacity. Risk is also evaluated using multidimensional assessment of physical risks, psychological risks, and social risks. Analysis of the three dimensions yields an overall risk assessment for a client's situation as low, moderate, or high. Holistic assessment of the client helps the worker to recognize that strengths in one area of functioning can compensate for deficits and weaknesses in another.

The capacity–risk model has been used in practice as a conceptual tool for assessing older adults and their living situations. In addition to assessing the capacity of the client, the model evaluates the level of risk in the client's living situation. The correlation between capacity and risk is used to differentiate among adequate, marginal, and inadequate functioning. The model helps social workers differentiate between situations in which older adults are exercising their rights to self-determination, including the right to determine their own risk-tolerance level, and situations that require protective interventions.

It posits that when functioning is adequate (capacity high; any level of risk), no interventions are warranted. When capacity is inadequate (low capacity; high risk) social worker should pursue protective interventions; when capacity is marginal (moderate capacity; moderate risk) it is appropriate to pursue interventions that are geared toward increasing capacity and reducing risk. Part Two provides more detailed information on assessing capacity in social work practice with vulnerable older adults.

CHAPTER 4

Value Issues and Ethical Dilemmas

Social workers who work with vulnerable older adults invariably encounter ethical dilemmas in their practice. They are often challenged to reconcile their clients' values and preferences with values and assumptions of family members and others who may refer an older adult to an agency for help. Geriatric social workers are usually one of several disciplines involved in providing professional services and supports to older clients. It is not unusual to encounter situations in which physicians, nurses, psychologists, social workers and allied health professionals are all involved with the same client. In cases that involve complex health, mental health, and psychosocial issues, these professionals may collaborate, share information, and reach consensus during the diagnostic and evaluation stages of developing a comprehensive assessment only to encounter difficulties getting clients, families, health and mental health professionals, and other service providers to agree on the goals and preferred outcomes for treatment and interventions.

In some instances, professionals from different disciplines may work together in one agency, as members of an interdisciplinary team. These teams are likely to have established protocols for how the team reconciles differences and arrives at recommendations for treatment goals and plans. In other instances, the multidisciplinary team may represent professionals in independent practices or from different agencies. These practice and organizational arrangements can further complicate the process of arriving at professional recommendations about treatment goals and plans. Different professions may have different perspectives, ethical values, and practice codes. It is not unusual for clients, family members, and various professionals to disagree and to encounter difficulties reaching consensus about the best treatment goals for a particular client. For social workers, the NASW *Code of Ethics* offers a set of values, principles, and standards to guide decision making and conduct when ethical issues arise (NASW, 1999). The capacity–risk model was developed by the authors as a conceptual scheme that reflects the NASW values embodied in the *Code of Ethics* and can be used to apply social work knowledge, core values, and ethical principles to making informed, ethical decisions when working with vulnerable older adults. The authors advocate an empowerment perspective that emphasizes the strengths and resilience of older adults, even when they face physical and psychological challenges. The model promotes a client-centered approach to social work practice, while recognizing the rights, obligations, and responsibilities of others who may be involved or affected by decisions made about a client's care.

The social work values presented in NASW *Code of Ethics* (NASW, 1999) and summarized in Greene, Cohen, Galambos, and Kropf (2007) are reflected in the capacity–risk model. The six core values are as follows:

1. *Service:* Service to others takes precedence over self-interest. The capacity–risk model encourages social workers and other professionals to provide services to those who need it most—vulnerable older adults who are at-risk, even when the older adult is refusing help. The needs of the vulnerable client take precedence over the social worker's desire to work with clients who want to work with them.

2. *Social Justice:* Advocate for the rights of clients, particularly the most vulnerable in society, and pursue social change when indicated. The capacity–risk model was developed to support social workers in their advocacy efforts with vulnerable older adults. Promoting use of the capacity–risk model will support the pursuit of social change in competency determinations taking place in community, organizational and policy settings.

3. *Dignity and Worth of the Person:* Treat people courteously and in a caring manner, and respect individual differences as well as cultural and ethnic diversity. The capacity–risk model was developed to support an older adult's right to self-determination and promotes seeking interventions that are least intrusive and show respect for the client's values and culture.

4. *Importance of Human Relationships:* Hold relationships among people in the highest regard, and recognize that those relationships may be catalysts for change. Importance of the client–social worker relationship and the power of the therapeutic alliance when working with vulnerable older adults is a fundamental principle of the capacity–risk model. In addition, the value of enhancing supportive relationships and promoting efforts to enlarge social networks for older adults who are socially isolated is incorporated in the model.

5. *Integrity:* Be mindful of the profession's mission, values, ethical principles, and standards, and apply them in practice. The capacity–risk model was developed to assist social workers in applying social work values and principles in challenging situations involving at-risk older adults who refuse interventions. The model helps social workers recognize potential conflicts of interest and maintain ethical standards in practice with this population.

6. *Competence:* It is your obligation to increase your professional knowledge and skills and use them in practice. The primary goals of the capacity–risk model is to educate social workers on assessing capacity in older adults and guiding social work assessment and intervention decisions for use in practice with vulnerable older adults.

One benefit of using the capacity–risk model as a conceptual scheme for ethical decision making in complex problem-solving situations involving vulnerable older adults is that social workers are clearly able to articulate their rationale, knowledge base, values, and the ethical principles they use to arrive at decisions and recommendations for practice in these cases.

A second benefit of using the capacity–risk model is that it provides a common language and concepts that can facilitate dialogue and understanding during supervision, consultations, and interdisciplinary team sessions. Although the capacity–risk model is a useful and empowering tool for ethical decision making, advance care planning strategies can increase the likelihood that older adults maintain control of decisions about their care, even if they experience decline and losses in their ability to clearly communicate their wishes.

AGEISM

The majority of older people maintain their ability to function independently throughout their lives, despite medical conditions and chronic illnesses that are more prevalent among older adults. Yet we live in a society in which discrimination against people based on physical characteristics, including age, race, and gender, persists. Ageism continues to influence how older people are treated and can affect their access to opportunities, services, and resources. In addition to physical characteristics, social circumstances can create additional sources of inequity in how people are treated. For example, there are situations in which people who are married enjoy more rights than those who are single, widowed, or divorced; homeowners may have access to protections of assets and respect for privacy that are not available to renters; individuals with more education may be better able to negotiate complex healthcare systems; and older adults with higher incomes may have access to more options and choices about long-term care arrangements than low-income seniors. Social workers are required to engage in culturally sensitive practice; this includes being aware and sensitive to ways in which professional practices and social policies can exclude and unjustly affect older adults. One example of how older people are inadvertently disadvantaged is reflected in the policies of the Medicare program, the primary health insurance program for people who are elderly and disabled. For many years, the social work professional has been represented among advocates for equal coverage and copayment requirements for outpatient treatment of physical and mental health conditions. Medicare beneficiaries were historically charged 20 percent copay for physical health services, but 50 percent for mental health care. Advocacy efforts have resulted in passage of the mental health parity act (in 2008), equalizing the copay for medical and mental health services. Yet disparities remain. Many mental health practitioners "opt out" of participation as providers and do not accept direct payment from Medicare for their services because of low reimbursement rates and costly and cumbersome administrative requirements. These problems are particularly problematic in their impact on access to mental health services for older adults. Social workers in private practice and other mental health practitioners frequently decide that they do not have the capital and administrative infrastructures to afford to accept direct reimbursement from Medicare.

As noted by a posting from the Association of American Physicians and Surgeons (n.d.):

> It is simple to opt out of Medicare—far simpler than staying in the Medicare program. Hundreds of physicians have already opted out, and we [have] not heard a single regret by any of these physicians. Once CMS unleashes its dreaded new program of "private auditors" to shake down physicians in the Medicare program, far more physicians will likely opt out—and even more will wish they had.

A consequence of this and other problems with the primary health insurance program for older adults is that low-income seniors who are not able to pay out of pocket for services and assume individual responsibility for seeking reimbursement from their insurance carrier have fewer options and less access to outpatient mental health care than those with higher incomes. Consistent with the social work *Code of Ethics*, social workers who practice with older adults have ethical responsibilities to the broader society, including a responsibility to "engage in social and political action that seeks to ensure that all people have equal access to the resources . . . they require to meet their basic needs and to develop fully" (NASW, 1999, p. 23); also, "social workers should act to expand choice and opportunity for all people, with special regard for vulnerable, disadvantaged, oppressed, and exploited people and groups" (NASW, 1999, p. 24).

AUTONOMY AND INDEPENDENCE

Some of the myths and stereotypes about growing old challenge customary assumptions about the rights, dignity, autonomy, and independence of adults, particularly during the advanced stages of old age. Within families, adult children sometimes anticipate that a "role reversal" will occur, resulting in adult children assuming parentlike roles while their parents will assume a dependency role. Some professional service providers, including geriatric social workers, elder law attorneys, and financial planners, market their services to adult children in ways that perpetuate the assumption of universal dependency and role reversal in later life. Medical providers in busy inpatient and outpatient settings sometimes find it quicker and easier to discuss medical options with adult children, to rely on adult children to "translate" and communicate with the older patient, and to relay the older patient's choices and decisions to the medical team, much as parents did when obtaining medical care for their children. In addition to "role reversal," the myth and stereotype of aging as a "second childhood" persists in many settings, especially in unenlightened institutional long-term care settings. Some of the names for aging programs were borrowed from names used in children's services, such as adult day care, sitter services for adults, and adult foster care. "The institutionalization of ageism in later life is reinforced by the legal, political, educational, health and welfare structures of modern society. Ageism is also internalized in the attitudes of individuals towards older people" (Bond & Corner, 2004, p. 65).

In a qualitative study of how older people respond to ageism, Lynn Corner characterized three distinct groups: (1) the empowered; (2) reluctant collaborators; and (3) the dominated or oppressed (Bond & Corner, 2004). Empowered older people were those for whom control and autonomy were central. These individuals recognized the need to be involved in decisions that affected their lives and struggled against being devalued because of their age. "In their encounters with health, social caregivers and family they maintain control and negotiate their independence; they challenge institutionalized ageism and demand that they be treated as individuals with needs and rights" (Bond & Corner, 2004, p. 73). Reluctant collaborators are frustrated by their inability to control aspects of their lives but reluctantly accept their situations because they perceive few other options; "they conform while being aware that ageism was experienced in their interactions with health and social providers as well as family and friends" (Bond & Corner, 2004, p. 73). Dominated or oppressed individuals have a sense of fatalism about their conditions and a belief that little could be done. These individuals are likely to underreport symptoms and accept change and decline as normal attributes of aging. Dominated or oppressed individuals don't challenge the negative stereotypes of old age.

The NASW (1999) *Code of Ethics* addresses the value of social justice and the ethical principle of working with and on behalf of vulnerable and oppressed individuals and groups. In working with older adults, this means being proactive in supporting the rights of empowered older adults; being aware of and sensitive to opportunities to empower those who are reluctant to exert their rights; and being proactive in requiring that professional colleagues treat older people with dignity and respect and respect their rights to "socially responsible self-determination" (NASW, 1999).

RESISTANCE TO ACCEPTING HELP

Social workers who practice in public agencies (such as adult protective service programs and community mental health centers) and those in nonprofit agencies supported by grants from public organizations (such as programs funded by state offices on aging) often receive referrals of older clients who are not seeking help for themselves, but for whom others initiate the request for assistance. Communities around the country grapple with questions about how to get help for vulnerable older adults who do not self-identify as needing services, especially those who do not have families involved in providing support and assistance. In our increasingly mobile society, families may not live in the same state as their older relatives and may be unaware of changes in their relatives' ability to manage their care. Older people who experience decline in their ability to independently manage the demands of daily living because of physical, emotional, social, financial, or mental health problems, and who do not have family or an adequate informal support network to address their care needs, are often at risk for neglect and failure to obtain services to adequately address their basic human needs. These "at-risk" clients are often referred to agencies that employ geriatric social workers. Older adults who are referred by others for community services are often unfamiliar with social work services and sometimes fearful of losing their privacy, autonomy, and independence. These factors can contribute to older adults being resistant to accepting help.

Older clients who are "at-risk" and resistant to accepting help present challenging dilemmas to social workers. In these situations, social workers are faced with an important professional and ethical dilemma: when to intervene against the older person's will and when to respect his or her right to self-determination. Abramson (1985) defined "self-determination" as the freedom to act as one wishes, using the abilities and resources necessary to fulfill one's purposes with freedom from coercion and interference.

Any discussion of interventions with resistant clients must include an examination of ethical issues, as the mere idea of attempting to provide assistance to someone who does not want help creates an ethical dilemma. An ethical dilemma exists when one can cite justification for taking either of two opposing courses of action. An ethical dilemma is a situation in which one is unsure about what is right or what is good, or when there is a conflict between opposing moral systems or obligations (Abramson, 1985; Conrad & Joseph, 2006). In working with older clients who are "at-risk" and resistant to accepting help, social workers are faced with the ethical dilemma of exploring the potential need for protective services versus respecting an individual's right to autonomy, self-determination, and privacy. Resolving these situations requires careful consideration of individual and professional value systems and mastery of professional knowledge and skills for working with this population.

Equally important is a discussion of values. Values refer to individual or shared conceptions of what is desirable or good. Values are influenced by culture, social learning, and life experiences. As a consequence, values vary across individuals, groups, and communities. In working with clients who are resistant to accepting help, it is important for professionals to be aware of their individual values, their professional values, and the implicit and explicit values of the agencies and communities in which they work. In addition, understanding a client's value system can be critical to understanding their resistance to accepting help and for making appropriate decisions about when and how to intervene. Awareness of the value system of others within the client's environment, such as family and neighbors, can also help to clarify conflicting perspectives and competing thoughts about appropriate options and outcomes for problem solving.

One of the cornerstone values of the social work profession is respect for the client's right to self-determination. An emerging issue in geriatric practice is this: "Who is my client?" Changing demographics and mobility trends have created multigenerational families that may be spread over large geographical distances. Social workers who engage in practice with long-distance family caregivers have to make a conscious effort to ensure that they avoid interventions that infringe on the rights of the older people, particularly when the older person is not present and involved in seeking help. Because the capacity–risk model is client centered, it guides social workers to give support, enhancing and maximizing clients' rights to self-determination while respecting the rights of others when developing and recommending care plans.

The following sections examine common scenarios in which geriatric social workers encounter ethical issues when working with vulnerable older adults.

RECONCILING DIFFERENCES IN CLIENT AND FAMILY VALUES

Adult children often seek services on their parents' behalf, sometimes identifying problems and needs that the older adults denies; or the older adult may prefer to address his or her problems and needs without help from agencies or people outside the family. Adult children frequently have to balance the needs, demands, and preferences of multiple generations, including their children, spouses, siblings, and parents. Situations can be further complicated when there is more than one adult child and the adult children disagree about decisions and plans. Although few older people live with their adult children, most have children and grandchildren who are involved in their lives. In fact, family members are the major source of support for older adults. Eighty percent of informal care for older adults is provided by family members (Kelly, 2008). Because older adults are intricate parts of family systems, competent geriatric social work practice requires that social workers develop knowledge and expertise for assessments and interventions with individual older adults as well as with their family systems. These skills are critical for recognizing and reconciling value differences and addressing problems in family dynamics that may span multiple generations of the family life cycle.

HOSPITAL AND NURSING HOME ADMISSIONS

Over the past 25 years, there have been tremendous changes in healthcare delivery systems. With the advent of funding schemes that link reimbursement for hospital stays with admitting diagnoses and third party payers' assessment of "medical necessity," healthcare professionals often feel that they have limited autonomy and authority related to admissions, discharge, and insurance coverage decisions. Medical care systems, particularly emergency rooms and hospitals, can be relatively fast paced, complex, complicated, and confusing for most patients, particularly older patients. Many older patients would benefit from social work services during all stages of hospital stays. This is particularly the case for those who do not have family members available to assist with negotiating care.

Unfortunately, a growing number of hospitals are closing traditional social work departments and reducing the range of social work services offered, limiting the role to discharge planning. In some cases, even the discharge planning role has been absorbed into nursing case management departments, entirely eliminating the social work perspective from the multidisciplinary team. Networking and collaboration between hospital social workers and community social workers has tremendous potential for improving psychosocial assessments for medical decision making and continuity of care for older patients. The impact of involvement and collaboration from the community social worker expands when the older adult is receiving care in a hospital that does not offer any social work services. It is not unusual for hospitalized older patients to appear disoriented, confused, more functionally impaired, and dependent, simply as a function of being in a hospital rather than in the familiar environment of their own homes. Social workers who have worked with an older person in the community, prior to a hospital stay, can provide "longitudinal assessment data" that can help hospital social workers differentiate functional changes that are disease and illness related from those that are the results of difficulty making the transition from home to hospital—that is, difficulty coping with sudden environmental change.

It has been observed that a hospital stay is a trigger event for nursing home placement. The majority of nursing home admissions are from hospitals, rather than from community and home living environments. Sometimes, older patients are discharged from hospitals to skilled nursing facilities with the intention that the stay will be short term; these stays sometimes convert to long term. Although it is assumed that these long-term placement decisions are because of the need for institutional care, owing to the progression of an illness or chronic health condition, no one has looked at the influence of other factors, such as whether a patient's prehospital level of control could be described as empowered, a reluctant collaborator, or dominated or oppressed (Bond & Corner, 2004). Community social workers often find that their professional relationships with long-term clients are weakened; they lose control of care plans they have negotiated with clients, and are disempowered when their clients are hospitalized. There is virtually no social work research that addresses issues of sustaining the social worker–client relationship across practice settings.

RECONCILING ETHICAL DILEMMAS

The capacity–risk model is a useful tool for social workers who seek to ensure that older people are treated with dignity and respect, and that we recognize and respect their rights to socially responsible self-determination. For those older people who are not "empowered" by personality, life experiences, and ability to function as effective self-advocates, the values and ethical principles of the social work profession provide a mandate for social workers to be aware of the potential for older people to be victims of ageism, to be devalued, and to unnecessarily lose their rights to autonomy and self-determination.

PART TWO

PART TWO

CHAPTER 5

Importance of the Client–Social Worker Relationship

The development of the client–social worker relationship is the most important element for effective assessment and practice with vulnerable older adults. Although much of the literature on capacity evaluation for older adults focuses only on the assessment process, it is critically important to recognize that fear and distrust of professionals from social service agencies can affect an older adult's cooperation and presentation during the evaluation process. Social workers who attempt to conduct a capacity assessment without first gaining trust and allaying fears omit a critical first step. Establishing a relationship with the older client can be challenging and may require multiple contacts because frequently the request for help was initiated by someone other than the client. The quality of the relationship can improve the social worker's ability to gather accurate information for the assessment. It also encourages the client and the social worker to approach interventions as a team, in partnership with joint goals that can increase the probability of success. The objective is to establish a relationship that develops into a therapeutic alliance through which the social worker can engage and empower the older client to optimize his or her functioning and quality of life. In this chapter, we present strategies to consider when attempting to establish an alliance with a vulnerable older client, who may be resistant to working with the social worker.

VALUING THE THERAPEUTIC ALLIANCE: ROOTS IN SOCIAL WORK

Valuing the client–social worker relationship and the role the client plays in this collaborative effort is one of the founding principles of social work practice. Rogers (1942) recommended that social workers allow their clients to lead their initial

45

conversations as part of a client-centered approach that focuses on "starting where the client is." This strategy supports the development of the client–social worker relationship in a number of ways. It encourages dialogue that is necessary for establishing a rapport with the client. It also helps to balance the power differential in the relationship by allowing the client to set the course of the discussion, and it demonstrates to the client that the social worker respects the client, appreciates his or her time, and is interested in what the client has to say. The strengths model of social work practice identifies the relationship as a fundamental resource and essential to the helping process (Saleebey, 1992). Compton and Galaway (1994) recognize the relationship between the practitioner and the client as a necessary condition of social work practice.

THE THERAPEUTIC ALLIANCE: A POWERFUL TOOL WITH VULNERABLE OLDER ADULTS

Roberts-DeGennaro (1987) stated that therapeutic involvement is necessary to acquire in-depth knowledge of the client to assess needs adequately and facilitate the processes for meeting them. One achieves the therapeutic alliance (also referred to as the "working alliance" and the "therapeutic relationship") when the practitioner is able to engage with, and effect change in, the client through the power of their relationship ("Therapeutic Relationship," n.d.).

Described as the joining of a client's reasonable side with the practitioner's working or analyzing side, the therapeutic alliance consists of three parts: (1) goals; (2) tasks; and (3) the bond (Bordin, 1979; Gelso & Hayes, 1998). The client and practitioner together establish "goals," which generally stem from the client's presenting concerns. The next step is to develop "tasks," which help the client reach his or her goals. The "bond" forms over time from the trust and confidence that develops between the client and practitioner as they work on the tasks to bring the client closer to his or her goals.

Counseling, psychotherapy, and other clinical models of social work in various mental healthcare and healthcare settings have been effective in identifying the therapeutic alliance as a principal goal in practice. In these settings, social work practitioners develop and apply skills that help foster the development of a therapeutic alliance with their clients. Recognizing the value of working through the therapeutic alliance is also critically important for social workers who work in geriatric case management, residential care, medical social work, home care, protective services, guardianship programs, or other practice settings serving vulnerable older adults. Much of the literature on social work practice in these areas focuses on knowledge of resources and linkage with community services, coordination of care, monitoring of services, evaluation of risks, and the facilitation of support with the client's informal and formal networks. In addition to these skills, it is important for community-based social workers working with vulnerable older adults to develop skills and use techniques that help establish a therapeutic alliance.

The therapeutic alliance is a valuable tool for social workers working with vulnerable older adults. Working through the therapeutic alliance improves the social worker's access to accurate information, reduces the client's resistance to interventions or support services and generally results in better outcomes for the client. However, establishing the trust necessary for the therapeutic alliance can be particularly difficult when working with clients who are resistant to the social worker's help. In these situations, the social worker can focus on establishing a nonthreatening relationship that (although not a therapeutic alliance) is strong enough to allow the social worker to begin the assessment.

The social worker can use the assessment process itself as another vehicle to foster the development of a therapeutic alliance. Gathering assessment information provides the social worker an opportunity to spend time with the client, use dialogue as a tool, and attempt other strategies that can further strengthen the relationship. Collaborative conversations between the client and social worker can reveal client goals. As their relationship gets stronger, the client may be willing to work with the social worker on a nonthreatening "goal" (such as nutrition) and allow the social worker to coordinate a relatively noninvasive support service (such as home delivered meals), or the "task." The process of collaboratively working on tasks gives the client and social worker opportunities to establish trust and respect. The positive feeling that occurs when the client meets the goal can create a bond that empowers the client and social worker as a team. This "bond" improves the social worker's ability to further reduce the client's resistance to addressing more sensitive areas. As the client and social worker identify more goals and carry out tasks (or interventions) to meet these goals, they strengthen their bond even further, fostering the formation of the therapeutic alliance. The social worker can use concrete tasks as a vehicle to initiate the process of collaboration that fosters the development of the therapeutic alliance. This collaborative process is depicted in Figure 3.

Figure 3: Process of Collaboration to Foster the Therapeutic Alliance

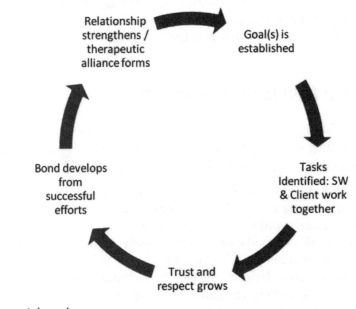

Note: SW = social worker.

THE THERAPEUTIC ALLIANCE REQUIRES A RELATIONSHIP

Although many therapists are highly skilled at implementing strategies to foster the therapeutic alliance, less attention is often given to skills that help to establish the initial relationship. In therapeutic settings, many clients are self-referred, asking for the appointment, and seeking a good relationship with their therapist. Sometimes the client has requested a particular social worker based on the recommendation of a friend or family member and therefore some level of trust has been established even before their first meeting. Other times, the client is motivated to work with a particular practitioner because he or she is a provider accepted by the client's health insurance.

Achieving a therapeutic alliance can be more difficult in community-based practice with vulnerable older adults. These clients often do not ask to see a social worker, do not recognize the value of working with a mental health professional, or are not interested in the services offered. This challenge increases when the client also has some level of cognitive impairment and may not be able to appreciate his or her own limitations or the social worker's potential to provide assistance. Literature on social work practice with involuntary clients provides some guidance in areas such as reducing client resistance and gaining trust. However, these strategies pertain to working with clients who are in settings such as prisons, community parole programs, juvenile delinquency programs, substance abuse programs, or other involuntary mental health or court-ordered situations.

Community-based practitioners attempting to engage a vulnerable older adult may not have the opportunity to implement these strategies because, in contrast to involuntary settings, these social workers often do not see the older adult at regularly scheduled (albeit mandatory) meetings. Vulnerable older adults living in the community generally have the ability to close the door and refuse to see the social worker. As a result, the initial steps attempting to engage the older adult in conversation (and encourage them to agree to see the social worker again) become critical if there is to be a client–social worker relationship at all.

RELATIONSHIP-BUILDING STRATEGIES

Successfully establishing a relationship with vulnerable older adults is challenging, particularly when they are resistant to accepting services. We have identified eight relationship-building strategies for work with this population:

1. Appreciate time with the client—use dialogue as a tool.
2. Be dependable, positive, and respectful to the client.
3. Attempt to understand the client's resistance.
4. Seek opportunities to balance the power differential and foster trust.
5. Be nonjudgmental and nonthreatening.
6. Be flexible and consider carrying out "nonclinical" tasks.
7. Be persistent, be open to rejection, and keep trying
8. Seek supervision or peer consultation.

Appreciate Time with the Client—Use Dialogue as a Tool

Meaningful conversations between two people who share a rapport often result in the establishment of a relationship. "Rapport" is a term used to describe the comfort level felt when one person perceives the person with whom they are talking as understanding the person, or being "on the same wavelength" ("Rapport," n.d.). To establish a rapport, the social worker needs to have an opportunity to spend time with the older adult. This is an important point. Jumping to techniques used in the therapeutic alliance, or principles that help transition a relationship to a therapeutic alliance, are not effective if the social worker is not able to engage the client in meaningful discussions first. It is therefore important for the social worker to perceive opportunities to spend time with the client (during which they can encourage conversation) as a critical first step in the relationship-building process.

During initial conversations, more casual informal discussions of the client's life, experiences, and concerns should replace formal client interviews in which the social worker asks a host of questions about the client's demographics, health and mental health diagnosis, financial resources, family supports, or other areas typically listed on assessment gathering forms. Allowing the older client to lead the initial conversations and share what is important to him or her promotes dialogue and the development of a rapport (Rogers, 1942). Sometimes the clients are interested in talking about the past, sharing hobbies they enjoy, or discussing a favorite book or movie. Other times, the clients may prefer to ask the social worker questions, seeking to find an area of common ground. The topic of the dialogue is not as important as having the dialogue itself.

Finding opportunities to show the client empathy in early conversations can reduce clients' feelings of powerlessness, increase their sense of control, and improve their engagement with the social worker (Pinderhughes, 1989). If the older adult needs encouragement to talk, asking open-ended questions about nonthreatening topics may increase the client's comfort and willingness to engage in conversation. Cowger (1992) identified the strengths-assessment template as an effective tool for engaging a client in dialogue and assisting the client to tell his or her story. Some clinicians feel the extended time they need for these casual conversations is an inappropriate use of their professional role as "time is money." However, having informal casual conversations with a client does use interview skills. They are just used differently to foster a nonthreatening atmosphere for better communication (Tice & Perkins, 1996).

Be Dependable, Positive, and Respectful to the Client

To establish respect and trust with the client, it is important to be dependable, arranging regular appointments to see the client and following through on agreed-on items. Continually changing visits, missing scheduled home visits, or visiting at the last minute when it fits into the social worker's schedule does not show respect or value for the older client's time. At times, the social worker may be the only contact the older person has. Allowing the social worker to visit may be a big step for the isolated older client who could view several missed appointments as validation that he or she should not have believed that the social worker really cared about him or her. The social worker also needs to present a positive attitude that is affirming toward the client, engage in active listening as the client articulates concerns, and talk candidly with the client about his or her behavior and interpersonal activities (Tice & Perkins, 1996). Maintaining client confidentiality and informing the client when and why confidentiality needs to be broken are important issues to address directly when establishing trust.

When meeting with the client in the presence of the client's family, conversations should be primarily directed to the older adult even if the adult child is considered the "responsible party." If the social worker is accompanying the client to see a doctor, it is important to encourage the physician to address the older adult directly, and, when necessary, structure responses in a way that identifies the client as the decision maker. Presenting the older adult as the primary person whom the social worker is assisting (rather than the social worker as the expert to whom the contact should be directed) helps to balance the power differential and demonstrates to the client that the social worker respects him or her as an adult, rather than viewing the client like a child.

Attempt to Understand the Client's Resistance

Many vulnerable older clients referred to a social worker do not perceive themselves as having problems or needing the assistance that others have requested on their behalf. It is important to understand resistance from the client's perspective to effectively establish a relationship that will work with this population. Some of the "at-risk" clients who come to the attention of agencies are "elderly orphans," who do not have close family members to help with and plan for care needs (Soniat & Pollack, 1993b). At other times, family members may feel that they have exhausted their ability to help and are unable to convince their relative to accept outside assistance. Some have a distrust of strangers that keeps them from accepting help if the helpers or professionals are also the "strangers." Others fear loss of privacy and control. Gerontology research has consistently documented that, when in need of help, older people turn first to family and their informal network. Older adults turn to formal services only as a last resort (Krout, 1985; Tennstedt, Harrow, & Crawford, 1996).

Understanding a client's value system can be critical in understanding his or her resistance and in making appropriate decisions about when and how to intervene. The value system of others within the client's environment (such as family or community) may also add to resistance of "social services." When working with clients who are resistant to accepting help, it is important for professionals to be aware of their individual values, their professional values, and the implicit and explicit values of the agencies and communities in which they work. Within U.S. society, there is a strong adherence to the value of independence. Many people feel that accepting help from social service agencies means giving up independence and acknowledging deficits, weaknesses, or personal failure. Culture, social learning, and life experiences influence values. As a consequence, values vary among individuals, groups, and communities.

Seek Opportunities to Balance the Power Differential and Foster Trust

To encourage the establishment of trust, there needs to be a balance in the power differential between the social worker and the older client. It is important for the older client to feel at least as an equal (and sometimes the expert) with regard to his or her relationship with the social worker. The social worker may need to look for ways to demonstrate how much he or she values and respects the older client, as well as find ways to give the older client control. Focusing on clients' accomplishments, emphasizing their potentials, and reinforcing their strengths is one way to demonstrate respect for clients and establish a positive line of communication (Tice & Perkins, 1996).

Allowing the client to lead the initial interviews is one way the social worker can give the client more control. This shifts the social worker's focus from asking questions to gather assessment information to participating in dialogue in which the client determines the content. If the older adult will not allow the social worker in his or her home for the initial interview, but is willing to meet in the lobby or at the neighborhood coffee shop, meeting with the client at the client's preferred location can also help to even out the power.

Be Nonjudgmental and Nonthreatening

Remaining nonjudgmental is critical when working with vulnerable older adults who may have impairments, and who may already be wary or resistant to accepting assistance from others. The social worker's home visit can reveal a lot of information about the older client. Sometimes the social worker may enter a house full of items and papers that leave only a pathway to walk. The social worker may detect the smell of urine or feces and realize the older adult has been trying unsuccessfully to manage incontinence. Perhaps during the home visit, the older client offers a cup of tea and the social worker follows the client into the kitchen to find rotting food and bugs everywhere. When working with this population, it is important that the social worker be prepared for such events and does not show shock, disgust, or great alarm.

Immediate intervention would certainly be appropriate in situations that present an imminent threat to the client's life, such as discovering there is no heat in the client's home and the client shows signs of hypothermia. Immediate intervention would be similarly appropriate if the social worker found the client in a state of delirium from a life-threatening infection. However, if the situation does not pose imminent danger to the client, the social worker should show respect for the older adult, focus on their relationship, and look to address the issues in a calm and respectful way.

These situations can cause anxiety for the social worker who worries about the client's risk of falling, eating rotting food, or suffering bites from the bugs. It is important to seek supervision or consultation to help evaluate the factors objectively. Knowing how long the client has lived in his or her current environment and if there have been any recent changes helps distinguish an acute situation from a chronic one. In situations that are not imminently life threatening, the primary goal of the social worker should be to be nonjudgmental, show respect, and work on developing a relationship. Through the relationship the social worker will seek to carry out a comprehensive assessment and work with the client to implement interventions and effect change that help improve the client's quality of life.

Client Example: Ms. Miller

An older adult we call Ms. Miller has been living on her own for many years, is very independent, and has always refused offers of assistance from concerned neighbors. She has recently agreed to meet with the social worker to talk about her desire for transportation to the grocery store. On the first visit, the social worker finds Ms. Miller in dirty clothes that smell of urine, her hair matted, and bites on her face and arms that appear to be from bugs. There are rodent droppings throughout the house, and there appears to be no clean area for food storage or preparation. The situation alarms the social worker and she spends her time talking to Ms. Miller about the need to have the garbage removed and the bugs exterminated, or to consider moving into a new living arrangement. After leaving, the social worker returns to her office and immediately makes phone calls to set up heavy house cleaning, extermination of the bugs, food delivery, and other services for Ms. Miller.

Ms. Miller is upset that the social worker never addressed what she wanted to talk about (transportation). Ms. Miller feels disrespected by the social worker's reaction to the condition of her home and she fears the social worker may try to move her into a senior facility. She decides not to trust the social worker and plans to manage on her own as she has always done. The social worker calls to set up another appointment and is excited about all the services she has located, but Ms. Miller does not agree to meet with her or to consider these services.

Discussion: Once the social worker determined the client was not in an immediately life-threatening situation, the social worker should have focused on hearing what the older client was interested in, on establishing a relationship, and gently exploring other areas in addition to transportation that might have been helpful to the older client. Being nonjudgmental and nonthreatening is very important when working with this vulnerable population. This is difficult when facing situations that seem intolerable for any individual to endure. Reflecting on one's own personal and professional values and how they may affect one's response is important when working with this population (Soniat & Micklos, 1993).

Be Flexible and Consider Carrying Out "Nonclinical" Tasks

It may be necessary for clinical social workers to provide some concrete services or carry out "nonclinical" tasks to establish a relationship with a vulnerable older adult. Someone else who is worried about how a vulnerable older adult is managing at home refers the majority of those who come to the attention of social service agencies. Many of these vulnerable older adults do not view themselves as needing the help others have requested on their behalf. Although the older adult may not feel the need to see a social worker or have an "assessment," he or she may ask for help with a concrete need such as getting to the grocery store or reading through mail. Some agencies may respond to this initial refusal of case management and request for help to get to the grocery store by providing names of transportation services, volunteer drivers, or home care or errand assistance services. It is important to recognize a vulnerable older adult's request for help with an everyday task as a potential opportunity to develop a relationship. Engaging the senior in conversation to establish a rapport and develop trust can occur at the same time as a concrete service such a providing a ride to an appointment or picking up items from the pharmacy.

Concerns regarding whether the activity is an "appropriate role for a clinical social worker" are less important than having the opportunity to engage with the resistant client. It is an example of starting where the client is (what is important to him or her) and giving him or her control regarding how he or she will agree to see a social worker (even if the social worker serves as a driver and assistant). Reframing the service provided based on the social worker's goal to engage the older adult is helpful. Defining this time as clinical activity during which the social worker is attempting to develop a rapport, rather than focusing on the task or errand itself helps to clarify the purpose. It also serves to differentiate when it may be appropriate for a clinical social worker to serve in a nonclinical role such as driving a client to the grocery store versus assigning this to a friendly volunteer or companion. Social workers should discuss any circumstances in which they are considering acting outside their normal role with their supervisor to ensure they are functioning in an appropriate role and adhering to standard social work ethical practices.

Be Persistent, Be Open to Rejection, and Keep Trying

Sometimes when the social worker arrives, the older adult refuses to talk with him or her. Attempts at using the strategies discussed above fail. There is no request for any services or assistance that the social worker can respond to, and the older adult refuses to open the door and engage in any kind of dialogue. Some agencies may document that social work services were offered and refused and close the case. It will take a new referral, or a crisis, to expose the older adult to another offer of help. "Waiting for the crisis" is a well-known phenomenon for practitioners working with community-based older adults.

Providing more opportunities for the older adult to interact with the social worker may increase the likelihood of engagement and ultimately encourage the older adult to accept services, resulting in a better outcome. Opportunities to interact with the potential client can occur in many different ways. If the older adult refuses a traditional home visit, the social worker could be creative and consider alternative ways to engage the individual. For example, calling on the phone every couple of weeks to see how the person is doing can help to establish a rapport, some trust, and may lead to the older adult eventually allowing the social worker to do a home visit. If the older adult refuses both home visits and phone calls, try to identify alternative ways to reach out. Perhaps sending a card may produce a letter-writing relationship. Bringing a holiday gift basket or offering to provide a service like shoveling snow from the steps may be another way to make contact and begin a dialogue with the older adult. Once the social worker begins interacting with the older adult, he or she can consider other relationship-building strategies such as using dialogue as a tool or carrying out concrete services.

Sometimes a legal guardian requests a social work assessment, but the client still refuses to see the social worker. In the following example, the social worker's persistence fostered a relationship that ultimately became a therapeutic alliance.

Case Example: Mrs. Jones

Mrs. Jones, an 85-year-old woman who had no family or friends, appeared to be eccentric and had a history of severe mental illness. She was found to lack capacity and had had a legal guardian appointed by the court years ago. The guardian supported Mrs. Jones's stated desire to remain at home where she lived in fairly stable condition for several years. Mrs. Jones's health began to decline, causing impairments in her ability to manage her daily needs. The guardian's attempt to put in support services failed because Mrs. Jones's paranoia and other psychiatric issues made her unwilling to allow anyone in her home. The guardian did not want to remove Mrs. Jones from her home unnecessarily, especially because most senior residential care options would not be possible because of her behavior and psychiatric needs. The guardian was concerned about Mrs. Jones's well-being and was responsible to the court to make sure she was all right. The guardian hired a social work case management program to assess Mrs. Jones, monitor her status, and advise him when and if he needed to remove Mrs. Jones from her home.

Mrs. Jones refused the offer from the social worker to visit or talk on the phone. The social worker considered others ways to interact with her. Aware that Mrs. Jones went to the same restaurant in the neighborhood every day for lunch, the social worker decided to see her there. The social worker met with the owner of this restaurant (with the guardian's consent) to learn information such as Mrs. Jones's routine, contacts, and ability to manage in that setting. The social worker started eating at the restaurant once a week, sitting at the table next to Mrs. Jones. Over time, they started simple conversation. Mrs. Jones started to look forward to seeing the social worker, and after a few weeks agreed to let the social worker sit with her at her table. Although the social worker did introduce herself and explained what she did, the client's mental health issues and cognitive status impaired her ability to really understand why the social worker was seeing her. The social worker continued to go for lunch once a week as one way of monitoring Mrs. Jones and continuing to develop a relationship.

A few months later, the social worker received a call from the owner of the restaurant reporting that Mrs. Jones had not been there for several days. The social worker could not reach her on the phone and went to her house but could not get an answer at the door. The social worker then called for emergency services. The paramedics found Mrs. Jones on the floor where she had been for two days following a fall. Mrs. Jones was dehydrated and afraid. She did not trust the paramedics and refused to go to the hospital. When the social worker came forward, Mrs. Jones recognized her from their visits at the restaurant and felt relief to see someone she knew. With the social worker's support and offer to accompany her in the ambulance, Mrs. Jones agreed to go the hospital. While in the hospital, Mrs. Jones started receiving psychotropic medications to reduce her symptoms of paranoia, which also reduced her resistance to accepting help. The hospital physicians and discharge planners were then able to work with Mrs. Jones through the relationship of the community social worker and the authority of the guardian.

Discussion: In this example, working on developing a relationship was the initial intervention. The connection with the restaurant enabled someone to notice and contact help when she did not appear for several days. This probably saved Mrs. Jones's life. Furthermore, the relationship provided the reassurance Mrs. Jones needed to agree to go to the hospital where she received physical and mental health care. The same community social worker was ultimately able to get Mrs. Jones to agree to a discharge plan with home care and case management support. This was possible because Mrs. Jones's relationship with the social worker had developed before the crisis happened.

There are certainly ethical considerations regarding fostering a relationship without the client understanding the social worker's role and to what degree one can attempt to interact with someone who has refused services. In this situation Mrs. Jones had a severe mental illness and was already deemed unable to make her own decisions. Although the guardian consented to the services, the social worker still had to consider the client's capacity and the level of risk involved when taking steps that were against the client's stated wishes.

Carrying out the least intrusive and least restrictive intervention that is consistent with the values of the client is also important. In this case, the social worker determined that taking steps to provide some level of oversight and contact with Mrs. Jones (even though it was initially against her stated wishes) was less restrictive and less intrusive than closing the case. If the social worker closed this case, the guardian would have to consider more aggressive ways to ensure that Mrs. Jones was cared for, such as having marshals come to remove her from her home to place her into a senior facility. Difficult issues often present themselves when working with vulnerable older adults who are still making their own decisions, as well as those who have surrogate decision makers in place but who continue to want to live in the community. Seeking supervision or peer consultation to help discuss and balance the legal, ethical, and value considerations with the assessment of the client's capacity and risk is important.

Seek Supervision or Peer Consultation

Consulting a supervisor or peer consultant or, ideally, engaging in a team discussion, provides support for social workers facing the challenging situations and difficult decisions presented when working with vulnerable older adults who are at risk and resistant to accepting help. When attempting to establish a relationship with a vulnerable older client who has refused the social worker's offers, it is important for the social worker to be aware of and talk about his or her own feelings of rejection as well as issues with transference and countertransference. "Transference" is the unconscious redirection of feelings for one person (past or present) to another. The transference phenomenon can be compared to the feeling one has when someone says or does something that reminds him or her of the past, striking a nerve that creates an "emotional time warp" and transfers the person's emotional past and psychological needs into the present ("Transference," n.d.). In a clinical context, transference refers to redirection of a client's feelings from a significant person to the social worker, which can manifest itself in many forms such as rage, hatred, mistrust, extreme dependence, love, or placing the social worker in the status of an idol.

"Countertransference" generally refers to the social worker's emotional entanglement with the client or his or her feelings toward the client. These feelings may stem from an emotional reaction determined not by the client's own personality traits, but, rather, by the social worker's unconscious conflict (Jung, 1969). Similar to transference, in countertransference, the client's personality may strike a nerve with the social worker that reminds him or her of the past and creates an "emotional time warp," transferring the social worker's psychological needs and emotions related to another person in his or her life onto the client. Social workers' understanding of the client's transference and their attunement to their own countertransference help social workers regulate their own emotions. Recognizing the potential for unconscious feelings (such as those related to a parental figure) is particularly important, because facing feelings of rejection, inadequacy, or other similar emotions are common for social workers attempting to establish a relationship with a client who refuses to work with the social worker and is resistant to services.

When considering ways to engage the older adult, social workers should discuss with their supervisor or director any circumstances in which they are considering acting outside their normal function. Carrying out tasks for clients, accompanying clients on activities, or interacting with clients in other nontraditional roles can blur client–social worker boundaries. Evaluating these boundary issues, discussing potential transference–countertransference factors, and considering how practitioner or client values may be affecting decisions are important areas to address in supervision or peer consultation. The opportunity to examine these issues helps to ensure that the social worker is functioning in an appropriate role and adhering to standard social work ethical practices.

BARRIERS TO UTILIZING RELATIONSHIP-BUILDING STRATEGIES

There are operational barriers to implementing relationship-building strategies. Individuals, communities, and professionals have different values affecting the decision to serve clients who do not initially want the services. There are also implications for cost and questions regarding who would pay for the service. Third-party payers (such as an insurance company) who cover the cost of an assessment or case management often require the client's acceptance. Many private case management programs have a fee for the social work service. Older adults who do not want assistance are not likely to pay for the social worker's time to work with them. Thus, the cost becomes a barrier and relationship-building efforts usually end. At times, a family member or concerned friend may hire the case manager. Although this covers payment for the social worker's time, there are still ethical concerns regarding providing case management without informed consent, or spending time working on the relationship when the client does not know others are paying for it on his or her behalf.

Social work services covered by tax dollars also pose barriers. Although some communities cover case management services for older adults who are self-neglecting, the client usually still needs to agree to work with the case manager or be referred to adult protective services (APS). Clients who meet the criteria but who refuse APS and are not at imminent risk or clearly lack full capacity usually end up "waiting for the crisis" to resurface with APS.

Communities considering funding more staff time for work with resistant clients face questions regarding distributive justice. When spending tax dollars providing outreach to older adults who do not want the service takes funds away from another program, how does one decide which one to fund? Eliminating unwilling clients is one natural way to establish parameters regarding conditions under which tax dollars can be used to pay for staff time. However, even when these parameters are established, these vulnerable older adults still exist and continue to come to the attention of social workers in many settings.

SUMMARY

Establishing a relationship with an older client who is resistant to accepting social services is one of the most challenging tasks geriatric social workers face. Successfully developing the relationship enables the social worker to be more effective. This relationship can be cultivated into a therapeutic alliance, a powerful vehicle that improves the client's outcome. Despite the best of efforts, social workers and other community-based professionals often fail in their efforts to work with resistant clients and to prevent crisis situations because they were unable to establish such an alliance (Soniat & Micklos, 1993).

We promote the use of relationship-building strategies and advocate for more training opportunities on the use of the therapeutic alliance specifically for practice with community-based vulnerable older adults. The process of the assessment itself can foster the growth of the therapeutic alliance and significantly affect the quality of the evaluation as well as the success of interventions and the overall outcome for the older client. Research studies are needed to validate and quantify the impact of using these relationship-building strategies with older at-risk adults who are initially resistant to accepting services, compared with simply closing the case and waiting for the next crisis.

CHAPTER 6

Assessing Capacity

There have been significant changes in the types of settings in which social workers practice and the skill requirements for competent practice with older adults. These changes correspond with the increasing complexity of the geriatric landscape—settings in which older people live and receive care (G. D. Cohen, 1994). Older people historically lived in their own homes, with family, or in nursing homes. Today, living choices vary considerably; the new landscape for aging includes settings like congregate housing, assisted living facilities, life or continuing care communities, senior hotels, foster care, group homes, and a growing diversity of retirement homes and communities. Social workers typically worked with older adults in hospitals and nursing home settings. Today, social services for older adults have expanded into diverse practice settings from the private sector to nonprofit agencies and community programs funded by the Older Americans Act of 1965 (amended 2006), such as senior centers, day health programs, respite services for families, adult protective services, case management services, home health and home care services to support various living arrangements.

Over the past 10 years, the social work profession has received substantial support from the John A. Hartford Foundation (Hooyman, 2009) to better prepare leaders, social work educators, and researchers for challenging careers to improve and provide vital services to the growing population of older adults. One outcome of this initiative has been greater specificity in the core and advanced skills required for competent practice with older adults. The four core knowledge and skill areas are: (1) values and ethics; (2) assessment; (3) interventions; and (4) aging programs, services, and policies. Although specialized gerontology practice skills are required for competent practice with all older adults, specialized skills and competencies are especially critical for practice with vulnerable older adults. In chapter four we discussed the values and ethical issues that social workers encounter in practice with vulnerable older adults. This chapter addresses assessment of vulnerable older adults.

One of the more challenging areas of assessment that social workers encounter is capacity assessment. Social workers who practice with vulnerable older adults must be skillful in conducting capacity assessments. One study found that social workers identified client decision-making capacity as the most significant factor influencing their support of patient self-determination, especially when competent clients choose to remain in unsafe living situations (Healy, 2003). The social work profession's "person-in-environment" perspective and use of a comprehensive biopsychosocial–spiritual approach to assessment recognizes that functional capacity assessment includes not only a biomedical assessment of decisional capacity, but also includes consideration of risks in the individual's environment, the individual's lived experience, and his or her values and preferences. It is critical to recognize that one should not lose the right to take risks simply because one is old.

As noted by the late international gerontologist Daniel Thursz (1995):

> Despite a great deal of progress in the efforts to end the myths surrounding the aging process, there are still some powerful images that govern both policies and programs dealing with older people. None is more manifest than the view that older people are increasingly dependent, need protection from their environment, and eventually from themselves. It is this notion that creates enormous barriers to the development of policies based on the strengths of the individual and his or her right to self-determination.
>
> Clearly, there are older people who are frail, some of whom cannot make decisions for themselves. There are older people who need protection from exploitation by forces in society, sometimes from relatives and even from themselves. However, this is not the case with the overwhelming majority of older people who are not only capable of self-determination but insist on maintaining their independence and dignity, even in the face of physical difficulties. . . . They seek autonomy and participation in decision-making. They do not perceive themselves as clients or patients. They are not willing to abandon their judgment for the judgment of others and want to maintain control of their own destiny. (p. xi)

A social worker who practices with older adults may be the only social worker in his or her host setting. Services to older adults are often provided by interdisciplinary teams. In health settings, interdisciplinary teams are typically led by physicians. In community settings, nurses, lawyers, psychologists, and social workers may be legally recognized as appropriate disciplines to conduct capacity assessments. Social workers bring a unique perspective to capacity assessment by holistically examining the person within the context of his or her social environment and by assessing both functional capacity and risks. Whenever possible, social workers seek to avoid involuntary interventions with older adults by using their knowledge and skills to develop interventions plans that respect clients' right to self-determination, enhance and increase clients' capacity for self-care, reduce psychosocial and environmental risks, and thus help clients to avoid involuntary and undesired care options. Social workers strive to help clients develop care plans that are consistent with their values and preferences, respectful of the rights and limitations of others, and tolerant of levels of risk that are reasonable and acceptable to the client.

Competent social work practice with vulnerable older adults requires a high level of professional knowledge and skills. Professionals who have not had specialized geriatric training, supervised geriatric practice experience, and continuing education for practice with older adults have a responsibility to develop knowledge and skills for practice in this area. This chapter addresses that need by providing a conceptual model that social workers can use when there are questions about an individual's ability to exercise reasonable self-determination in making decisions about his or her care. The model is a conceptual tool for critical thinking about how to organize the biopsychosocial assessment data gathered during the assessment process. Applying the model requires that social workers master the underlying geriatric knowledge base for comprehensive geriatric assessment, which has many domain-specific assessment tools such as mental status exams, neuropsychological exams, and physical capacity assessments. Although some of these tools are used in this discussion, this text is not intended as a substitute for in-depth and ongoing education in understanding the underlying research, strengths, and weaknesses of the various domain-specific assessment tools.

HOME VISITS: CRITICAL IN CAPACITY EVALUATIONS

When assessing functional capacity in vulnerable older adults, it is important for practitioners to see the client in his or her home setting. The practice of home visits has always been a valued tool in the field of social work. Documentation of the merit of home visits was apparent as early as the 1880s, when social workers helped individuals living in the settlement houses (Berg-Wegwe, 2005; Netting, Kettner, & McMurty, 2004). Home visits are important for establishing a relationship, gathering critical assessment information, and developing appropriate intervention plans. When considering decisions regarding the client's ability to continue living at home, evaluating the client's level of functioning in his or her own home provides the most relevant information. The home setting provides cues that may assist the client to complete functional tasks successfully. The home may also present distractions or competing demands that can interfere with a client's abilities to perform everyday tasks. In comparison, functional tests administered in a medical setting do not have cues or distractions and may either underestimate or overestimate the client's ability (Grisso, 2003; Marson & Briggs, 2001; Marson & Ingram, 1996).

Changes in Physical or Mental Status

It is critically important for social workers to be alert to and aware of the significance of acute and sudden changes in physical and mental conditions of their older clients. While most older people have one or more chronic illness, any acute condition or change in the presentation of a chronic illness warrants immediate medical attention. Social workers may be the first to notice these changes or the first contact for clients or family members who are concerned about changes in medical conditions and whether they warrant emergency attention. Delirium, dehydration, toxic reactions to medications and other symptoms require immediate medical screening for treatable and potentially reversible symptoms that could become chronic and irreversible if treatment is delayed. The social worker does not have to know all the illnesses, disorders, potential side effects of medications or other factors that can affect capacity. However, understanding the common conditions that can impair function empowers the social worker to urge clients to seek appropriate medical attention to screen and treat reversible causes of impairment.

A wide range of medical and mental health conditions may affect functional capacity with aging. Some of these conditions may improve or resolve themselves with treatment or other interventions. Nutritional deficits, side effects of medications, substance use or abuse, depression, anxiety, and other disorders are examples of conditions that can cause functional impairments that may improve after treatment (Zarit & Zarit, 2007). Some diseases—such as hypertension, congestive heart failure, and diabetes—are often considered primarily for their effect on the older person's body, while the possible impact on the person's memory and, thus, function is overlooked (Garavaglia, 2008). Sensory impairment can reduce the client's ability to react safely to dangerous situations and may affect functional capacity.

A social worker's level of understanding of illnesses, conditions, treatments, medications, and their effects on an older person (who may have multiple, coexisting medical conditions) is important to consider prior to making decisions regarding interventions, especially involuntary interventions. Resolving potentially treatable medical and physical conditions can eliminate the impairments and enable the client to achieve a higher level of functional capacity. Once treatable conditions have resolved or improved, a new functional assessment should take place prior to judging capacity and making decisions regarding interventions. Often, after resolution of a medical condition, the client returns to a higher functional capacity, and involuntary intervention may no longer be necessary or appropriate. The effect on functional capacity when vitamin B12 deficiency is treated and resolved is depicted in Figure 4.

Decisional and Functional Capacity

When evaluating capacity, it is useful to distinguish between the concepts of decisional capacity and functional capacity. "Decisional capacity" (also referred to as "cognitive capacity") connotes having sufficient cognitive ability to make choices that reflect an understanding and appreciation of the nature and consequences of one's actions (Checkland & Silberfeld, 1993; Kapp, 1990; Silberfeld & O'Rourke, 1994). An individual has decisional capacity when he or she is able to receive and understand information and to formulate a decision based on that understanding. Decisional capacity is the basis of the concept of informed consent. It considers the person's ability to communicate a choice, to understand relevant information, to appreciate the medical consequences of the situation, and to reason about treatment choices (Applebaum, 2007).

"Functional capacity" includes decisional capacity but is a much broader concept. It involves evaluation of an individual's abilities and disabilities in the context of his or her physical, psychological, interpersonal, and social environment (Schogt &

Figure 4: Enhancement of Functional Capacity Through Treatment of Condition

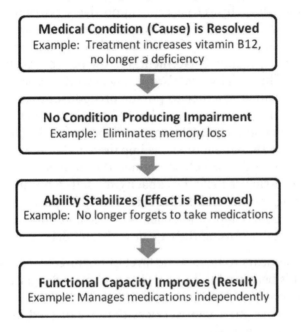

Sadavoy, 1987). Review of everyday skills and abilities that enable a person to live independently within his or her home and community occurs in a functional capacity assessment (Loewenstein & Mogosky, 1999). Because impairments in the person's ability to manage his or her needs may occur with or without corresponding declines in cognition, a comprehensive assessment that includes both decisional and functional capacity is most effective when evaluating an older adult's ability to continue living at home (Marson & Herbert, 2000; Royall, Chiodo, & Polk, 2000).

To assess functional capacity, social workers gather information from the client, his or her family, support network, and environment. As noted earlier, a therapeutic alliance with the client is essential for conducting an accurate evaluation of the client's capacity. Having the client's consent to communicate with other professionals who are providing care can improve the quality of the assessment. Professional collaboration with physicians, mental health providers, home health nurses, physical therapists, attorneys, financial planners, and other involved professionals creates an interdisciplinary team approach to assessment. Fostering a collaborative effort improves the social worker's ability to gather pertinent information and results in the most accurate assessment of the client's capacity.

WHEN IS CAPACITY ASSESSMENT INDICATED?

The conceptual model for capacity assessment described in this chapter was developed as a guide for social workers to use when considering whether or not to intervene with a vulnerable older adult who has some level of impaired capacity, who seems to be at risk for danger, harm, or negative consequences in his or her preferred living situation, and who refuses to accept supportive services that could potentially reduce the risk for harmful outcomes. For example, a hospital social worker may need to assess a patient's capacity to make discharge decisions when the medical team recommends nursing home placement, but the patient insists that he or she can safely return home. The social worker's assessment of the patient's functional capacity can be used to decided whether to pursue procedures that could result in legal appointment of a surrogate decision maker to authorize transfer of a client from a hospital to a caregiving nursing facility or to advocate for the client's right to decide to go back home even though he or she is impaired and may return to a risky situation. The conceptual model, which we named the *capacity–risk model*, guides the social worker in assessing the client's capacity for self-determination and ability to function in his or her home, and it identifies the appropriate level of intervention that may be warranted to support the client's choice and minimize risks.

Primary indicators for using the capacity–risk model are as follows:

- The client appears to have some level of impaired capacity.
- The client is perceived to be at risk for harm or danger in his or her current living environment.
- The client refuses to accept services that are offered or that could help to reduce or minimize risks.
- A decision has to be made about whether to respect the client's right to self-determination or to support an intervention plan that is not consistent with the client's stated preference.

CARRYING OUT A FUNCTIONAL ASSESSMENT

Because functional assessments measure the person's ability to carry out common tasks for daily living, they often provide the most relevant data to evaluate a client's capacity to live at home. More than 40 different functional assessment measures exist (Loeweinstein & Mogosky, 1999). These measures generally fall into three categories: (1) self-report and caregiver–informant report; (2) performance-based functional assessment; and (3) clinician rating measures. Kovar and Lawton (1994) provided a review of the main concepts for functional assessment and highlight the most effective tools, strengths, and weaknesses.

To achieve a functional assessment that is most reflective of the client's capacity, the social worker would seek to synthesize information from a number of different tools and sources. The Activities of Daily Living (ADL) Scale and the Instrumental Activities of Daily Living (IADL) Scale are two effective functional assessment tools that are the most commonly used with older adults (Angel & Frisco, 2001; Lawton & Brody, 1969; Loewenstein & Mogosky, 1999). The ADL Scale measures basic self-care skills such as eating, dressing, bathing, toileting, grooming, personal hygiene, ambulating, and transferring (Katz, Ford, Moskowitz, Jackson, & Jaffe, 1963). The IADL Scale involves more cognitively complex activities such as using transportation, doing laundry, obtaining and preparing food, maintaining shelter, handling finances, obtaining necessary medical care, making healthcare decisions, and administering medications (Duke University Center for the Study of Aging and Human Development, 1978; Wolinsky, Callahan, Fitzgerald, & Johnson, 1993).

When completing the ADL or IADL scales, the social worker rates the measures after considering information from several sources, including the client's self-report and information from family members, caregivers, or other qualified informants. During home visits, the social worker seeks opportunities to directly observe the client perform tasks as a way to add a performance-based measure. A physical or occupational therapist's evaluation can provide another performance-based functional assessment that can occur in the client's home, in a clinic setting, or both. Augmenting self- and informant-based measures with performance-based measures is more accurate than using one source alone (McCue, 1997).

EVALUATING PHYSICAL CAPACITY

When evaluating physical capacity, the social worker gathers medical, health, sensory, and functional assessment information. This includes areas such as the client's current medical concerns, treated and untreated illnesses, substance use, diet, medication use, and the client's ability to see, hear, smell, and touch. It is important to connect the client with an appropriate physician who can carry out a comprehensive physical exam. The client would ideally see a geriatrician or an internist who has experience in geriatrics and is knowledgeable about the common conditions that can affect an older person's health and function. Obtaining diagnostic information about the client's condition, prognosis, and treatment options is important for understanding the medical issues that affect the client. The assessment of physical capacity can reveal the presence of a medical condition (cause) that impairs the client, thus reducing the client's ability (effect), and lowering the client's functional capacity (result) (see Figure 5).

The capacity–risk model uses a "functional framework" that evaluates what the older adult is actually doing in particular situations in light of the unique demands in his or her environment (McCue, 1997). To assess physical capacity using the capacity–risk model, the social worker considers the client's functioning in the following areas:

Does the client

- obtain necessary medical care?
- manage his or her personal care needs?
- obtain meals that meet nutritional needs?
- manage his or her medications?
- ambulate and transfer?

Synthesizing assessment data, observations, and professional judgment, the social worker evaluates the client's physical capacity on each measure as high (does regularly without difficulty), moderate (does irregularly or with difficulty), or low (does rarely, with great difficulty, or not at all).

Figure 5: Impairment of Functional Capacity by Medical Condition

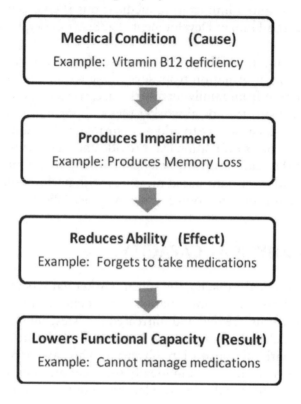

EVALUATING PSYCHOLOGICAL CAPACITY

The evaluation of psychological capacity begins with an assessment of the client's cognition. "Cognition" refers to thought processes that affect understanding. Cognitive thought processes include areas such as memory, association, language, attention, perception, problem solving, and mental imagery (Coren, Ward, & Enns, 1999). Whether a person has the cognitive ability to understand and make decisions forms a major part of formal capacity evaluations (Zarit & Zarit, 2007). There are a number of measures that have been developed to assess cognition. Folstein's Mental Status Exam (Folstein, Folstein, & McHugh, 1975) is one well-known tool that evaluates an individual's orientation to time, place, and person; memory; reasoning ability; abstract reasoning; reality testing; and judgment. Community social workers should be familiar with standardized mental status exams that screen for organic disorders such as dementia. When a client refuses formal psychiatric or neurological workup, the social worker can incorporate some components of various standardized mental status exams into informal interviews with the client. The social worker can also supplement formal cognitive exams with information gained from observations and informal interviews with the client or collateral contacts. For example, a social worker would assess for memory problems in a client who, for no other apparent reason, has his or her telephone or utilities disconnected because of failure to pay the bill. One should strongly suspect disorientation to place (a symptom of dementia or delirium) for a client who becomes confused about the location of his or her apartment.

There are many older adults with lifelong psychiatric issues that have never been formally evaluated, diagnosed, or treated. Social workers going into the home of a vulnerable older adult may be the first practitioners to screen the older adult for psychiatric conditions. It is important for the social worker to be familiar with standard mental health exams and the criteria used in the *Diagnostic and Statistical Manual of Mental Disorders* (4th ed., text rev.) (American Psychiatric Association, 2000). The social worker can identify areas that require further psychiatric assessment by administering the geriatric depression scale and other tools to screen for symptoms, such as depression, delirium, hallucinations, paranoia, anxiety, or mania. Identification and treatment of psychiatric disorders can improve the older adult's cognition and functional capacity.

Social workers, unfortunately, often face situations in which the older adult has not seen a doctor or refuses medical and mental health evaluations that could identify possible reversible illnesses. "At-risk" clients are often resistant or uncooperative with formal mental health examinations. Older people are underserved by the mental health system and often have very negative views about needing or using these services (Butler & Lewis, 1982; Lipsman, 1996). When a social worker needs to make decisions about intervention, he or she has to rely on available information. The capacity–risk model is a conceptual tool that can help to organize and make sense of the information that is available through standardized assessment tools, observations and professional judgment.

Assessing Psychological Capacity Using the Capacity–Risk Model

The capacity–risk model focuses on the impact the cognitive impairment or psychiatric illness has on the client's function, rather than the diagnoses or symptoms themselves. This is in contrast to traditional assessments of cognition—such as neurological evaluations, psychiatric evaluations, or neuropsychological testing—which are often measures of disease and disability rather than of the individual's functioning (McCue, 1997), and measure cognitive impairment such as "memory loss" or a diagnosis such as Alzheimer's disease. By contrast, the capacity–risk model looks not at "memory loss" per se but in the way it affects the client's behavior or ability to carry out activities.

Understanding the client's past lifestyle and value system is important in how the social worker perceives current behavior. For example, when working with a client who lives alone, does not leave the house, and has no regular contact with others, knowing whether the client is newly isolated or if he or she has always chosen to live as a recluse influences whether the social worker considers social isolation to be a problem. It is also important to consider the client's level of comprehension and if he or she is able to communicate a choice, understand relevant information, compare the risks and benefits of available options, and understand and appreciate the situation accurately.

To assess psychological capacity using the capacity–risk model, the social worker considers the client's functioning in the following areas:

Does the client

- understand the decisions he or she is making and their consequences, including the consequences of refusing help?
- manage finances and make financial decisions that reflect reasonable judgment?
- perceive realistically the capacity of informal helpers?
- exhibit behavior that is consistent with past lifestyle or an implicit, explicit or expressed value system?
- respond appropriately in emergency and non-routine situations?

Using the same method that was used to assess physical capacity, the worker synthesizes psychological assessment data, observations, and professional judgment to evaluate the client's capacity on each measure as high (does regularly without difficulty), moderate (does irregularly or with difficulty), or low (does rarely, with great difficulty, or not at all).

EVALUATING SOCIAL CAPACITY

Assessment of the client's social capacity includes obtaining information about the client's informal and formal support networks, strengths, values and culture, financial resources, and environment. A client's "informal support network" includes family, friends, neighbors, and others who regularly interact with or support the client. Gaining an understanding of the family history, dynamics, and the role the client played is helpful. The absence of supportive relationships or strained family relationships is also significant information. Exploring the client's current relationships and understanding the amount of assistance the support network can provide is important. The client's "formal support network" includes organizations of which the client is a member, such as a church, support group, or a club, as well as official groups or professionals working with the client, such as home care agencies, meal programs, volunteers, office on aging programs, structured housing staff support, mental health providers, or medical practitioners. The social worker would evaluate the current amount of support provided and explore the level of support available to the client in the future. If the client lives in a senior housing residence, the social worker would evaluate the amount of assistance provided as well as the level available to meet future demands as the client's needs change.

Obtaining information on the client's "strengths" provides information on experiences that may have empowered the client, such as a career position, role in the family, or reputation related to skills developed in a hobby. Discussions that shed light on the client's values or culture can give the social worker greater appreciation for why the client may be resistant to accepting services.

Assessing economic factors involves obtaining information about the client's work history, retirement situation, and "financial resources" including income, expenses, and assets. In some cases, the client or his or her family may not want to share specifics about finances. Gaining a general understanding regarding the range of the client's finances may be sufficient as long as it indicates the client's ability to pay for services or qualify for publicly subsidized programs and services. Specific financial data may be necessary to help the client apply for subsidized or other income- and asset-based services. If the client is resistant to sharing financial information, the social worker should proceed with the assessment and indicate how the lack of financial information may affect intervention options. While gathering financial information, the social worker should explore how the client handles payment of bills and other finances. Obtaining this information may provide insights regarding the client's inability to manage finances or potential exposure to the risk of financial exploitation.

Evaluating social capacity includes an "environmental assessment" to gather information about the client's current living situation and conditions. The social worker considers the type and amount of support available to the client and his or her access to supplies or services such as grocery stores, pharmacies, social activities, and transportation. In some cases, the climate in which the client lives may be important. For example, a client who lives in a rural community that receives significant ice and snow in the winter is likely to experience less dependable home care support because of caregiver transportation problems in poor weather.

Assessing Social Capacity Using the Capacity–Risk Model

Strengths in the areas of social support can compensate for deficits and weaknesses in other areas of functioning. For example, the presence of a strong caregiving system can compensate for deficits in the individual's physical or psychological capacity. Living in a supportive environment, such as a senior building, or near neighbors who offer support can lessen the impact of physical impairments. Having adequate financial resources to acquire services can make a difference in an individual's capacity to function within his or her environment despite other deficits.

To assess social capacity using the capacity–risk model, the worker considers the presence and amount of supportive resources in the following areas:
Does the client have

- an informal support system (such as family or friends) that recognizes and responds to the client's needs?
- a formal support system (through agencies, providers, or faith community) that recognizes and responds to the client's needs?
- a living situation and environment that meets the client's basic care needs and is consistent with the client's customary lifestyle?
- sufficient financial resources to provide for necessities?

Using the same method that was used to assess physical and psychological capacity, the worker synthesizes data on social factors, observations and professional judgment to evaluate the client's capacity on each measure as low (resource is not present), moderate (resource present, but inconsistent or not sufficient to meet client's needs), or high (resources available, and sufficient to meet client's needs).

ASSESSING OVERALL CAPACITY USING THE CAPACITY–RISK MODEL

The social worker combines the results of the physical, psychological and social capacity assessments along with professional judgment to determine the client's overall level of capacity (see Table 1).

Table 1: The Capacity–Risk Model: Capacity Indicators

	Level of capacity		
Physical Capacity: Does the client . . .	**High (does regularly without difficulty)**	**Moderate (does irregularly or with difficulty)**	**Low (does rarely, with great difficulty, or not at all)**
. . . obtain necessary medical care?			
. . . manage his or her personal care needs?			
. . . obtain meals that meet nutritional needs?			
. . . manage his or her medications?			
. . . ambulate and transfer?			

	Level of capacity		
Psychological Capacity: Does the client . . .	**High (does regularly without difficulty)**	**Moderate (does irregularly or with difficulty)**	**Low (does rarely, with great difficulty, or not at all)**
. . . understand the decisions he or she is making and their consequences, including the consequences of refusing help?			
. . . manage finances and make financial decisions that reflect reasonable judgment? ·			
. . . perceive realistically the capacity of informal helpers?			
. . . exhibit behavior that is consistent with past lifestyle or an implicit, explicit, or expressed value system?			

Table 1: The Capacity–Risk Model: Capacity Indicators *(Continued)*

Psychological Capacity: Does the client . . .	Level of capacity		
	High (does regularly without difficulty)	Moderate (does irregularly or with difficulty)	Low (does rarely, with great difficulty, or not at all)
. . . respond appropriately in emergency and nonroutine situations?			

Social Capacity: Does the client have . . .	Level of capacity		
	High (resource available and sufficient to meet client's needs)	Moderate (resource present but inconsistent or not sufficient to meet client's needs)	Low (resource not present)
. . . an informal support system (such as family or friends) that recognizes and responds to the client's needs?			
. . . a formal support system (through agencies, providers, or faith communities) that recognizes and responds to the client's needs?			
. . . a living situation and environment that meets the client's basic care needs and is consistent with the client's customary lifestyle?			
. . . sufficient financial resources to provide for necessities?			

Overall Capacity: Type of capacity	Level of capacity		
	High	Moderate	Low
Physical			
Psychological			
Social			
Overall rating			

Note: For each indicator, determine the client's capacity as high, moderate, or low.

Figure 6: Assessment of Capacity

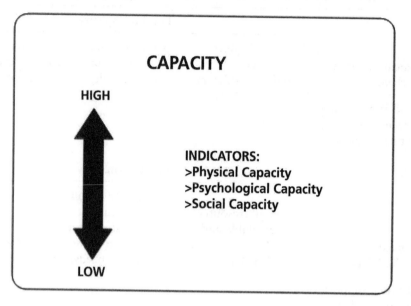

The capacity–risk model views capacity as a multidimensional concept. In contrast to an either–or criteria, the capacity–risk model recognizes that an individual's capacity can vary along a continuum from low to high. It also recognizes that the individual can experience limited or temporary incapacity as he or she moves up and down in the capacity areas as intervention or change takes place. At present, there is an unfortunate lack of a quantitative tools to facilitate the synthesis of biopsychosocial–spiritual data into a numeric measurement that reflects overall functional capacity. Nevertheless, using professional assessment skills, and, when available, team consultation, social workers can use the capacity–risk model to conceptualize functional capacity on a continuum from very low to very high. This continuum is shown as the capacity axis on Figure 6.

CHAPTER 7

Assessing Risk

In decisions about whether to intervene against a person's wishes, the concept of capacity has dominated professional decision making. There is growing recognition of the importance of adding risk assessment to the evaluation of an individual's capacity to make decisions and manage self-care. Including risk assessment helps the social worker determine whether the client has the capacity to function within his or her unique environment. Understanding the client's risk tolerance helps the social worker consider if the risks associated with a decision are acceptable risks for the client.

Frequently, clients who come to the attention of community-based agencies are experiencing risks from multiple sources. Understanding the specific risks in the circumstances of a client who is resistant to accepting help is essential. This chapter reviews concepts of risk assessment and presents the framework for risk assessment that is used in the capacity–risk model. The model promotes individualized assessment of risk using the biopsychosocial framework and measures that are consistent with the person-in-environment perspective.

THE GROWING DEMAND FOR RISK ASSESSMENT

The practice of risk assessment has been a function of adult protective services (APS) for decades. APS workers routinely screen for risks and, when appropriate, implement services to reduce risks.

The evaluation of risk was recently identified as a critical component for clinicians to include in reports submitted to the court for guardianship hearings (Moye, Wood, et al., 2007). Whether it is practitioners providing clinical information in guardianship cases, adult protective service workers investigating reports of suspected neglect, or community case managers, more social workers are seeking tools to guide them on evaluating risk and its impact on decision making for clients who are vulnerable older adults. When considering tools available to evaluate risk, it is helpful to first consider the concepts involved in risk assessment.

RISK CONCEPTS

- *Risk:* the probability or chance that harm, injury, danger, or loss will occur unless some action is taken; the possibility of loss or injury; the potential for unwanted, adverse consequences to human life, health, property, or the environment (Brearley, 1982).
- *Objective risk:* the difference between actual outcome and expected outcome. Probability of objective risk can be determined by measuring outcomes in previous cases involving similar situations. Actual risk can only be known after the fact for a specific case (Brearley, 1982).
- *Subjective risk:* a psychological uncertainty that stems from an individual's mental attitude (influenced by values, culture, and life experiences) and state of mind (influenced by knowledge and capacity for knowing); contains elements of uncertainty and doubt (Brearley, 1982).
- *Risk tolerance or acceptability of risk:* a value judgment; determined by personal and societal values. This is a likely source of variance between worker and client.
- *Probability or likelihood of risk:* subjective judgment; the degree of certainty that an outcome will occur unless some action is taken.
- *Severity of risk:* amount or extent of harm, injury, danger, or loss that is likely to occur.
- *Risk of alternative options:* Actions to prevent, reduce, or eliminate risks may have unintended consequences that create a new set of risks.

One of the difficulties of evaluating risk is that there is no clear agreement regarding what constitutes risk, risk factors, or how to measure them. Galantowicz and Selig (2005) presents risk as a combination of individual circumstance, events, and perception (or risk tolerance) in which an individual's risk tolerance is influenced by his or her expectations and preferences. Thus, what constitutes risk for one person can pose little or no risk for another. Many social work practitioners look to APS programs, policies, and tools for guidance on risk assessment in vulnerable older adults. Most states have APS laws that require them to balance the duty to protect impaired citizens with the civil rights of the individual citizen. APS policy in the state of Virginia defines "adult at risk" as an adult who "is in an endangering situation that may result in imminent injury, death and/or loss without the provision of adult protective services." The Code of Virginia defines "emergency" to mean that an adult is living in conditions that present "a clear and substantial risk of death or immediate and serious physical harm to himself or others." Thus, APS in Virginia focus assessment on risk with imminent or immediate consequences.

Many of the existing tools evaluating risk to vulnerable older adults measure risk based on the presence of risk factors such as memory loss. The Los Angeles

Risk Assessment Instrument identifies risk factors that consider the client's abilities and behaviors, financial resources, environmental factors, support factors, frequency and severity of abuse factors, and, if appropriate, alleged abuser factors (County of Los Angeles Community and Senior Services, 2005). Screens for risk factors are very helpful to guide the social worker in considering the broad range of potential causes of risk in a client's situation.

ASSESSING RISK: THE CAPACITY–RISK MODEL

The capacity–risk model conceptualizes risk from a functional perspective that considers the negative outcomes associated with risks, rather than just the presence of risk factors or risk behaviors. For example, a home care agency may hesitate to provide services to a client who has a diagnosis of dementia and who lives alone, based on the perception that doing so enables or perpetuates a high risk, unsafe living situation. Assessing risk from a biopsychosocial perspective guides the worker to consider the potential negative consequences of the living situation. Specifically, what negative outcomes does the worker fear that would affect the client's physical health? What negative outcomes does the worker fear that would affect the client's emotional or psychological health? Are there potential negative consequences in the client's living situation that would affect the client's social well being? To evaluate risk, the social worker considers information gathered from the referral source, the client, and other collateral contacts to assess what "types of risks" are present, how likely these risks are for this client, and the "degree of risk" associated with each risk factor.

Risk is considered unique to each client's circumstances. When evaluating risk, it is important for the social worker to consider the client's values and preferences and how this may affect the person's perception of risk or the person's perception of the negative outcome. A client's psychosocial history can provided insights on his or her risk tolerance level. The social worker should consider any historical data or evidence that is available to evaluate the client's history for risk tolerance versus risk-aversion decisions.

TYPE OF RISK

Risk is conceptualized as the potential for a negative consequence due to a variety of factors such as the client's environmental conditions, functional limitations, or psychiatric disorders. To evaluate the type of risks present in the client's situation, the social worker may use traditional risk screening tools that identify risk factors, such as those developed by the Los Angeles APS programs. After identifying potential risk factors, the social worker reframes the question to consider whether there is a potential negative consequence that may result from the risk factor. In this manner, many of the tools that screen for risk factors can be used with the capacity–risk model. Take, for example, a client who is found to have wandering as a risk factor. To evaluate the potential for risk using the capacity–risk model, the social worker considers the negative consequences of wandering—for example, is the client likely to suffer physical or emotional trauma from getting lost? There are three types of risk: physical risk, psychological risk, and social risk. We discuss each of these in the following.

Physical Risk

The first sphere for risk assessment within the biopsychosocial framework is evaluating physical risk. Physical risk is determined by the presence of negative consequence caused by physical, sensory, or functional limitations, such as the client's inability to carry out an activity of daily living or instrumental activity of daily living. Social workers should use this model along with other clinical judgment to determine if the client's physical risk is low, medium, or high. To assess physical risk using the capacity–risk model, the social worker considers the presence of risk in the following areas:
    Is the client at risk for

- malnutrition, starvation, or dehydration?
- hypothermia or hyperthermia?
- serious health consequences or physical decline because of untreated or mismanaged medical conditions?
- injury because of fire, gas leak, or other hazards caused by functional limitations?
- serious injury resulting from a fall?

Psychological Risk

The next step for risk assessment within the biopsychosocial framework is to evaluate psychological risk. Psychological risk is determined by the presence of negative consequences caused by organic, emotional or behavioral disorders such as dementia, depression, or schizophrenia. For example, if a client is confused and has memory loss, how does this affect him or her? What are some of the behaviors caused by the memory loss, and what are the potential consequences? Perhaps this client gets confused about where to store food and often forgets to put items requiring cold temperature in the refrigerator. Although the risk factor is memory loss, the capacity–risk model guides the social worker to focus on the effects of memory loss, such as the physical risk of disease or serious health decline because of unsanitary conditions. In another example, a client has depression and is not eating. In traditional screens, the risk factor would be positive for depression. The capacity–risk model guides the social worker to focus on the effect of the depression. If the depression is causing the client not to eat, the client is at risk of serious health consequences due to an inability to meet nutritional needs because of mental health problems. Social workers should always be alert to the potential risk for suicide among older adults, a factor associated with severe depression. Social workers should use this model along with clinical judgment to determine whether a client's psychological risk is low, medium, or high. To assess psychological risk using the capacity–risk model, the social worker considers the presence of risk in the following areas:

Is the client at risk for

- disease or serious health decline because of unsanitary conditions (for example, a senior who has hoarding behavior)?
- physical or emotional trauma from getting lost (for example, as a result of wandering)?
- injury or harm resulting from nonpayment of bills because of memory loss (for example, utilities turned off; consequences of unpaid taxes; loss of insurance because of unpaid health, home, or car premiums)?
- serious health consequences because of inability to meet needs resulting from mental health issues (for example, depression)?
- psychological or emotional trauma because of mental health problems (for example, emotional trauma from untreated anxiety)?
- psychological or emotional trauma because of an inaccurate perception of what is going on in his or her environment (for example, intense fear caused by delusions or paranoia)?

Social Risk

The third sphere for risk assessment within the biopsychosocial framework is evaluating social risk. Social risk is determined by the presence of negative consequences caused by social, interpersonal, and environmental factors. One risk factor for socially isolated clients is the potential for falling and not being found or assisted for days. The capacity–risk model guides the worker to consider the specific likelihood of this risk factor for a specific client. Specifying individual risks can help the worker to consider recommendations and interventions that could eliminate or minimize each specific risk. When considering social, interpersonal, and environmental factors that can negatively affect the client, the social worker may want to consider these questions: Are there stressful, exploitative, or abusive relationships with family or informal network? Is the client socially isolated, without the availability and support of a care giving system? What is the condition of the client's dwelling, and are essential utilities available? How safe is the neighborhood of the client? Social workers should use this model along with other clinical judgment to determine if the client's physical risk is low, medium, or high. To assess social risk using the capacity–risk model, the social worker considers the presence of risk in the following areas:

Is the client at risk for

- isolation?
- homelessness?
- grave injury or death from nonresponse in an emergency?
- harm from abuse or neglect by another?
- reduction of financial resources from exploitation or crime?
- destitution—no resources?
- harm caused by unsafe residence, unsound structure, or inoperative utilities?

- emotional trauma or cognitive decline resulting from a change in environment (for example, severe depression or confusion after placement in nursing facility)?

Once the social worker has determined the type(s) of risk to the client, the next step is to consider the degree of risk.

DEGREE OF RISK

Clients are frequently exposed to risks from multiple sources. It is often the cumulative effect of such exposures that changes the situation from one that was manageable or tolerable to one that is considered critical and requires outside intervention. To assess the degree of risk, it is usually helpful for the social worker to consider the following types of questions:

- What are the risk factors in a particular client's situation?
- Is there such a thing as acceptable or safe risk?
- How long have the risk factors been present?
- What, if anything, is different about the situation now in comparison with the recent past?
- What are the potential consequences associated with each risk factor?
- How significant are the potential consequences for the client? For others?
- What is the likelihood that the consequences will occur if the individual continues to refuse to accept help?

The "degree of risk" is determined by the amount of anticipated harm (severity of risk) and the certainty that negative consequences will occur (probability of risk), with probability estimated by evaluating the frequency of past similar events. Degree of risk can range from high (serious harm, with almost certain probability that the negative event will occur) to moderate or low risk (minimal potential harm, with a small probability that the negative event will occur). The social worker considers each type of risk (the negative consequence), attempting to understand the severity of effect on the client and the probability that this event will occur by considering the frequency of past similar events.

Degree of risk can range from high (serious harm with almost certain probability that the negative event will occur) to moderate or low risk (minimal potential harm with a small probability that the negative event will occur). The social worker considers each type of risk (the negative consequence), attempts to understand the severity of impact on the client, and the probability that this event will occur by considering the frequency of past similar events.

Severity or Impact of Risk

All people take risks. However, risks have different severity levels and the impact of the negative event (the effect) differs from client to client. For example, two clients have unsteady gait and are a fall risk. The social worker considers the consequence of serious injury resulting from a fall. The severity is determined to be higher for one client who has osteoporosis with a history of multiple fractures than for the other client who has strong healthy bones. In this case, the overall risk is higher for one client because of the severity, not the probability. The evaluation of risk should allow for variations based on each unique individual's situation, values, or life history. Isolation for an individual who has been socially active and connected his or her entire life carries a greater negative impact than it does for an individual who has lived as a lifelong recluse.

Probability of Risk

There are a number of sophisticated ways to define probability that consider estimates based on the number of times a negative event has occurred. Most of these estimates are based on the number of negative events that occur within a large group. For example, the probability risk of getting cancer if you smoke is determined by studies that look at a large group of smokers over a period of time and then document the number of individuals diagnosed with lung cancer to determine the percentage of probability. Probability measures used in group studies do not translate to evaluating the probability of a risk for an individual based on his or her unique situation. Counting the number of times a negative event has occurred is not possible on an individual basis—the occurrence of one negative event alone could result in the client's death.

Similar challenges faced engineers who were asked to present the probability of a negative event that, if it occurred once, would be catastrophic (such as failure in a nuclear plant). When basing probability on the number of times the negative event occurred was not practically possible, the engineers used the frequency of past similar events to determine probability. This approach can also be applied to assess the probability of a risk (negative consequence) occurring for a vulnerable older client, with the social worker looking at the frequency of past similar events to determine probability. For example, a social worker is attempting to determine the probability of a client being harmed by a fire in her home. To evaluate probability, the social worker would look beyond how many fires the client had started and include similar events or indicators such as behaviors that almost resulted in a fire. The presence of cigarette burns in the couch, signs of burned cookware or smoke-stained areas around the stove, and burned personal items or wax spills resulting from the client frequently knocking over candles are a few examples of similar incidents that would suggest a higher probability of the client being harmed by a fire.

PUTTING IT TOGETHER

To conceptualize the client's total amount of risk, the social worker would consider the "degree of risk" for each "type of risk" to determine if they have low, medium, or high risk.

For example, the social worker identifies the client to have a type of risk: physical risk of malnutrition, dehydration, or starvation. To determine the degree of risk, the social worker would consider the probability of this occurring by identifying the frequency of past similar events. In this case, the client was hospitalized for dehydration several months earlier and recently the client has felt weak, fainted several times, and exhibited periods of confusion possibly from being dehydrated. On the basis of this history, the social worker determines the level of probability of the client becoming malnourished, starving, or dehydrating as moderate to high. Then the social worker considers the level of severity of the risk and the impact on the client. The severity in this example is high, as it can cause death. But the social worker would also evaluate the impact of that on the client, which can vary on the basis of individual circumstances and beliefs. One client may feel death from dehydration constitutes a very serious negative consequence. Another client who is terminally ill may not measure the consequence of death from dehydration as severe. In the second case, the client may view a consequence such as a fire, which has the potential to destroy their home and belongings as more severe or grave than death.

Social workers faced with challenging decisions regarding a client's right to accept risk must evaluate the impact of risk as a factor unique to each client situation. For example, an 85-year-old man we call Mr. Kelly is physically healthy and ambulatory. Mr. Kelly has a dementia causing some memory loss and fluctuating disorientation. Mr. Kelly lives alone in a small apartment building that has fewer than 10 units in total. The building has one entry and exit and has front desk staff who are required to buzz all residents in and out 24 hours a day as a security measure for the apartment building. The client is well-known to the front desk staff and the other residents of this apartment building. Mr. Kelly has lived in the neighborhood for many years. He has always enjoyed walking to do his errands, spend time at the local library, and eat at his favorite lunch spot.

On several occasions in the past year, while Mr. Kelly was out in the neighborhood, he became disoriented, got lost, and could not immediately report his home address. Mr. Kelly agreed to recommendations for a companion during the day hours to accompany him on errands and provide assistance as needed. This has worked well for Mr. Kelly who has sufficient resources to cover the cost. The companion leaves after dinner when Mr. Kelly usually watches his news programs and goes to bed. Mr. Kelly has recently become more disoriented to time and on several occasions has prepared to leave the apartment building in the evening and night hours when he mistakenly thought it was time to meet friends for lunch. On these occasions the front desk staff have informed him of the time and redirected him successfully back to his apartment. A recommendation was made to expand the companion care to a 24-hour live-in to address the wander risk. Mr. Kelly refused, as he prefers not to have anyone living with him and does not want to lose the current companion, with whom he has a good relationship and who is not available as a live-in. Although Mr. Kelly has the resources to cover the current companion, the cost of covering two companions for 24 hours a day (rather than the live-in rate) would deplete his resources quickly. Concerned family who live out of state requested an evaluation regarding the client's ability to continue living in his apartment.

For many risk tools, Mr. Kelly would score high as a wander risk. He is disoriented to place and time, he is ambulatory, and he has a history of wandering. A social worker evaluating the level of risk to Mr. Kelly using the capacity–risk model

Figure 7: Assessment of Risk

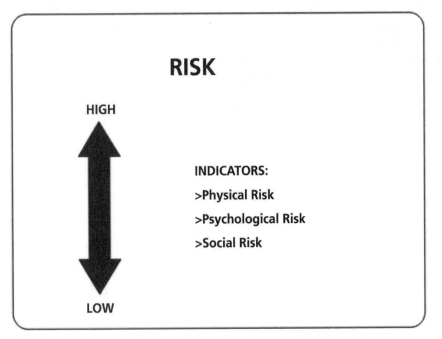

would consider the wander risk from the perspective of the potential harm from wandering. Does Mr. Kelly have the risk of experiencing physical or emotional trauma from getting lost, and what is the probability that this will happen? Using this framework, Mr. Kelly has a low risk for physical or emotional trauma of getting lost if he is wandering during the day because his companion is with him to keep him from getting lost, and if he is wandering during the evening and night hours, the front desk security staff protect him from leaving the building and redirect him to his apartment. Although there is still risk (perhaps a substitute front desk staff person does not notice his picture taped to alert them not to let him leave) that Mr. Kelly does leave and get lost, and although Mr. Kelly may be a "wander risk" and have a high probability of wandering in the neighborhood or within the apartment building, the risk of harm to Mr. Kelly is low, and the probability of Mr. Kelly actually getting lost is low. Thus, on this one indicator, the capacity–risk model's focus on impact rather than behavior affects the assessment of risk.

OVERALL RISK

As previously noted, clients who come to the attention of community-based agencies are frequently experiencing risks from multiple sources. It is often the cumulative effect that changes the situation from one that was manageable or tolerable to one that is considered critical and that requires outside intervention. Understanding as completely as possible risks involved in the circumstances of a client who is resistant to accepting help is essential. A determination of the individual's overall level of risk is made by synthesizing the types of risk and the degree of risk. At the present time, we lack a quantitative tool to facilitate this synthesis of data. Thus, using professional assessment skill, and when available, professional team consultation, the level of risk can be conceptualized on a continuum from very low to very high. This continuum is shown as the risk axis in Figure 7.

When evaluating intervention options, the social worker should consider new risks that may be connected to the intervention itself and try to avoid introducing equal or greater risks than had been there previously.

CHAPTER 8

Using the Capacity–Risk Model to Guide Assessment and Intervention Decisions

Social workers unfortunately often face situations in which there is less than optimal assessment data available to thoroughly evaluate a client's capacity and risk. Vulnerable older adults tend to be poor historians, so the history of medical and psychosocial problems may not be known. Sometimes a vulnerable older adult may not have seen a doctor in years and will refuse medical evaluations. Family and friends may not be aware of the details of a client's medical and psychosocial history. Although it is not ideal, the reality is that the social worker may have to evaluate a client's functioning with relatively limited assessment data. Using the capacity–risk model helps the social worker to be clear about the implications of the assessment factors that are present and about how these factors affect the client's ability to function.

For example, a social worker has been asked to evaluate an older adult's capacity by his adult daughter. The daughter is concerned about her father, who is living alone at home. This past year he has not been bathing regularly, his diet has been poor, and he has fallen several times on the stairs. The daughter recently received a call from her father's neighbor, who became concerned when he saw her father at the local grocery and heard him asking directions home because he was lost. The daughter visits her father every Sunday and noticed during one visit that his medication box was in disarray. She offered to help him fill the box, and he refused. The daughter feels it is time for her father to move into a facility where he would be safe and would receive regular medical and personal care and meal services. Her father will not consider a move or any help in the home and states he is fine. The social worker recommends a comprehensive medical, psychiatric, and neurological workup to look for changes in medical conditions, affects of mismanagement of medications, nutritional deficits, depression, and other things that could cause the father to become more confused, disoriented, and less functional. The father refuses any medical, psychiatric, or neurological workup and is resistant to engaging with the social worker to consider alternative solutions to address his daughter's concerns about his safety. This situation meets the criteria note in chapter 6 for use of the capacity–risk model:

- The client appears to have some level of impaired capacity.
- The client is perceived to be at risk for harm or danger in his or her current living environment.
- The client refuses to accept services that are offered or that could help to reduce or minimize risks.
- A decision has to be made about whether to respect the client's right to self-determination or to support an intervention plan that is not consistent with the client's stated preference.

CAPACITY–RISK MODEL FOR ASSESSMENT OF OVERALL FUNCTION LEVEL

The capacity–risk model is a conceptual tool that helps the social worker to synthesize assessment data and to reach an overall evaluation of a client's functional level. By reflecting on the assessment of the client's capacity (high, moderate or low) and the assessment of the level of risk in the client's living situation (high, moderate, or low), the social worker is able to conceptualize the client's functioning as adequate, marginal, or inadequate. This is determined by analyzing the relationship between the client's capacity and the client's risk. A graphic tool (see Figure 8) helps social workers apply the concepts of the capacity–risk model to integrate assessment data.

If a social worker assesses a client's capacity as high and his or her risk as low, the capacity–risk model indicates that the client's functioning is adequate. If a social

Figure 8: Capacity–Risk Model for Assessment

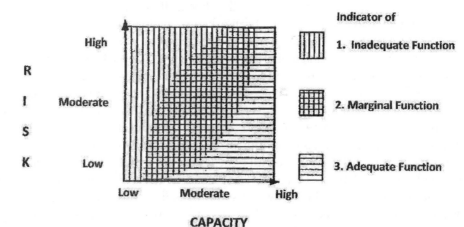

Source: Soniat and Micklos (1996).

worker assesses a client's capacity as moderate and his or her risk as moderate, the capacity–risk model indicates that the client's functioning is marginal. Using the capacity–risk model, a social worker would conclude that a client's functioning is inadequate when the assessment data shows that the client's capacity is low and his or her risk is high.

The capacity–risk model is a conceptual model that helps the social worker to organize and make sense of assessment data. The focus is client centered and is consistent with the person-in-environment (PIE) approach of social work.

INTERVENTION

Following assessment, the next question facing the worker is what, if anything, should be done. Usually, when working with "at-risk" resistant clients, the worker has only two options: involuntary interventions or respecting the client's right to refuse services. The latter option often means doing nothing, despite an intuitive awareness that the individual's situation will worsen without any interventions. At some point, the case will "resurface" or be referred again, most likely at a time of crisis. The phenomenon of "waiting for the crisis" is well known to protective services and other community workers.

The capacity–risk model offers a third option, psychosocial interventions, for at-risk clients with impaired capacity. Psychosocial interventions are geared toward encouraging clients to accept help and providing help that is geared toward increasing capacity and reducing risk. Using concepts from the capacity–risk model, the clinician evaluates the correlation between capacity and risk to determine what level of intervention is warranted (see Figure 9).

Figure 9: Capacity–Risk Model for Intervention

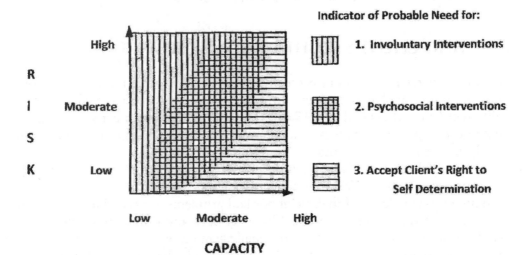

Source: Soniat and Micklos (1996).

CAPACITY–RISK MODEL FOR INTERVENTION

The following premises of the capacity–risk model guide decisions about interventions with clients who are resistant to accepting help:

Intervention Principle 1

When capacity is high, the individual has a right to self-determination and a right to refuse services, regardless of the level of risk present. No additional attempts to establish a relationship with the resistant client or his or her network is warranted.

Intervention Principle 2

When capacity is moderate and risk is moderate, social workers should attempt to establish a relationship with the client and client system. If a relationship is established with the client (or client system), the social worker should use psychosocial interventions that are geared toward increasing capacity and decreasing risks. The goal of services should be to increase capacity while reducing or eliminating risks. Appropriate interventions include those geared toward relationship development, strengthening the informal social network, enhancing the individual's capacity, and risk-reduction strategies.

Intervention Principle 3

When capacity is low and risk is high, social workers have a responsibility to provide protective interventions. These interventions may be involuntary, such as petitions for guardianship or referral for adult protective services. The social worker should attempt least-restrictive alternatives that are most consistent with client's values and preferences. The primary goal of intervention is to reduce the client's risks for physical, psychological, or social danger and harm.

ACCEPTING CLIENT'S RIGHT TO REFUSE SERVICES

Some situations referred to adult protective services (APS) agencies and other community programs involve older people who may be eccentric or have lifestyles that are different from others (Adams, 1996). Community workers must be careful not to attempt to impose their values or a community's values on an older person who is simply exercising his or her right to be different. For example, an elderly individual may be a lifelong social isolate who chooses not to socialize or even be friendly with his or her neighbors. This may concern neighbors who worry that no one visits and no one would know if their neighbor had problems or needed help. The concerns and perceived "risks" expressed by neighbors and others who might refer older clients in situations such as this are usually genuine and well meaning. In addition, community services such as friendly visitors and telephone reassurance calls may be available to reduce some of the potential risks of situations like this. However, if the client's capacity is high, community workers must accept an individual's right to decline services despite the level of risk presented.

INVOLUNTARY INTERVENTIONS

Situations in which a client's capacity is low and risks are high typically require involuntary intervention. These situations may involve circumstances of imminent harm or danger, but more often involve long term, chronic conditions that have become worse over time. Appropriate interventions might include obtaining emergency medical treatment, emergency psychiatric intervention, or petitioning the court for appointment of a legal guardian or conservator. There is wide variation among states' mental health and APS laws. Professionals who work with "at-risk" older people must learn the laws and legal procedures that apply to the jurisdictions in which they practice. In all instances, workers should pursue the least-restrictive alternative. An effort should be made to pursue interventions that are most consistent with the client's values and stated preferences when involuntary interventions are warranted.

PSYCHOSOCIAL INTERVENTIONS

The concerns by "at-risk" clients who lack the capacity to make decisions and manage their care needs can be overwhelming. Social workers are often confronted with demands from neighbors, apartment managers and other concerned people that they "do something." Involuntary interventions are not appropriate for situations in which the resistant client has moderate capacity and moderate risks. Yet the professional can do more than close the case and wait for the next crisis to occur. Instead, the social worker should continue to work on establishing a relationship with the client or the client system. Establishing a relationship or a therapeutic alliance with resistant clients is essential for effective work with this population. Despite the best of efforts, community workers often fail in their efforts to work with resistant clients and to prevent crisis situations because they are unable to establish such an alliance with clients.

Sometimes, regardless of the time and effort spent, workers are unable to develop a therapeutic relationship with the client and may be able to intervene through others, such as the informal support network. Through the relationship, either with the client or informal network, the worker aims to reduce the client's resistance, and implement interventions that increase the client's capacity and reduce risk.

Capacity Enhancement Strategies

Capacity enhancement and risk-reduction principles seek to improve the individual's ability to function independently while also decreasing the perceived risks associated with a client's situation.

Capacity enhancement principles include the following:

- Establish a therapeutic alliance with the client.
- Engage the informal support system in the intervention.
- Identify a "problem for work" that is reflective of something the client wants, even if the client cannot or will not articulate his or her needs.
- Set realistic goals.
- Pace interventions; allow adequate time to gain client's trust.
- Use informal networks, as appropriate, to enhance the client's capacity.
- Use formal services and community resources, as appropriate, to enhance client's capacity.
- Continue interventions until client is no longer at risk.

Risk-Reduction Principles

Risk-reduction strategies can guide a social worker in determining how to proceed. The approach incorporates the principles of "least restrictive alternative" and "maximum client involvement."

The eight risk-reduction principles are as follows:

1. Identify risk factors.
2. Prioritize risk factors, specifying the most serious or imminent risk, the second most serious or imminent risk, and so forth.
3. Develop a plan for reducing or eliminating each identified risk factor.
4. To the maximum extent possible, involve the client in implementing a plan for reduction or elimination of the most serious or imminent risk.
5. When the most serious or imminent risk cannot be reduced or eliminated through worker–client interaction, involve appropriate members of the informal network.
6. When the most serious or imminent risk cannot be reduced or eliminated through worker–client or worker–client–informal network interaction, involve appropriate formal system.
7. Following resolution of the most serious or imminent risk factor, apply procedures 4 through 6 toward reduction or elimination of the second-most serious risk factor.
8. Continue to implement risk-reduction plans, using strategies outlined in procedures 4 through 6, until all moderate and high risk factors have been eliminated.

CLINICAL EXAMPLE

A woman we call Mary arrived in Washington, DC, last fall after leaving Philadelphia, where APS had placed her in a boarding home after she had been evicted from her apartment for not paying her rent and seeming not to be able to live independently. Mary was a very small and frail woman with an unsteady gait and a hunched back; she weighed about 80 pounds.

The manager of the hotel where Mary was staying referred her to a senior service agency as he was concerned about her apparent inability to care for herself, exhibited by the demands she made of his staff. In addition, he and other staff members were concerned for Mary's safety as they had witnessed her asking strangers on the street for rides and assistance in carrying her things including her purse, both during the day and late at night. Mary wanted help in finding an apartment in a particular area that cost no more than $250 a month. She refused to accept that there was no place that would charge such a low rent and rejected all other housing options. Mary was disoriented to time and place and exhibited poor judgment and insight.

It was the end of December, and a dangerous cold front had just moved in. Mary was evicted from the hotel for nonpayment and became homeless. Mary refused to believe that the hotel could evict her and became angry and combative. Many hours later, she finally agreed to go to a shelter. Mary spent the next year moving from shelter to shelter while receiving support and assistance from several community agencies.

On several occasions, Mary admitted herself to a hospital as she was quite frail and had pneumonia from being out on the streets. The social worker at the hospital was unable to develop a satisfactory discharge plan as, again, Mary would accept nothing less than an apartment for $250. She refused placement in any senior assisted-living or other community housing program. Mary's health continued to decline, and she developed more problems taking care of herself. During her last hospitalization, the hospital felt it was unsafe for Mary to be discharged to a regular shelter. Two psychiatric evaluations were done as they sought to place her in a safer setting. Both psychiatric evaluations found Mary to have the capacity to refuse care. Mary eventually signed herself out of the hospital against medical advice and returned to the street.

Mary expressed to several people that she was cold, hungry, and needed help and did not understand why no one would help her. During the next year, the community social worker had sporadic contact from Mary who did not stay in any consistent shelter or maintain contact with the case management program. Mary's health continued to decline as her frailty and respiratory conditions were exacerbated by being homeless during the winter. In the late fall, the hospital contacted the community social worker, informing her that Mary has been admitted again. Although concerns regarding her health and safety remain, Mary continues to refuse the hospital discharge planner's recommendation to consider a more protective senior care residence. On the basis of psychiatric evaluations supporting her decisional capacity, the hospital plans to allow Mary to sign herself out against medical advice and return to the streets.

The community social worker questions why Mary has been found to have the capacity to refuse assistance. Although Mary can reason well, she believes a false premise to be true no matter what facts say otherwise. Although Mary performs well enough on the cognitive and mental status examinations administered at the hospital, she is unable to function well in providing for her own needs (functional capacity versus decisional capacity). The community social worker requests another assessment on capacity but also recognizes the psychiatric evaluation in the hospital settings will have limited access to how Mary functions in the community. After consultation with her team, the social worker recognizes the importance of her role as the community social worker in providing an assessment regarding Mary's functional capacity in the community. The social worker decides to use the capacity–risk model to guide her assessment of Mary's function. To use the capacity–risk model, the social worker will evaluate data to assess Mary's functional capacity and level of risk.

As is often the case with community social workers asked to intervene with a vulnerable older adult who is refusing support services, the social worker does not have all the assessment data that would be ideal to know to evaluate Mary's capacity. However, a decision regarding whether to initiate a petition seeking the appointment of guardian for Mary or other protective interventions needs to be made. Thus, the social worker applies the capacity–risk model, using as much information as is available from as many sources as possible. A summary of the information the social worker gathered regarding Mary follows.

Mary is physically frail, has difficulty walking with a cane, and cannot manage steps. Getting up from chairs is difficult, and Mary has a history of falls. Mary has chronic pneumonia, causing shortness of breath and fatigue. Mary is homeless and does not have regular nutrition, medications, or medical care. Her eyesight is poor, and she has difficulty managing tasks that require reading or writing. Mary often wears the same clothes, rarely bathes, and appears unkempt. Difficulty walking and managing steps makes public transportation difficult. As far as cognition, according to the psychiatric exams done at the hospital, Mary scores well enough on the Mini-Mental State Evaluation and other cognitive exams to have decisional capacity to make informed consent (and to sign herself out of the hospital against medical advice). However, Mary does have some impairment in understanding her options and reality—that an apartment in the upper northwest area of Washington, DC, is not available for $250 a month as she wants and can afford. Furthermore, Mary lacks an understanding of her own impairments and does not understand that she does not meet the criteria for independent living that is required by the low-cost senior housing in the area. The social worker also observed that Mary exhibits difficulty understanding and managing her finances and on several occasions has paid too much cash for items without realizing it.

Mary has no family or friends who are involved with her care. Since eviction from the hotel, Mary has had no fixed address. Attempts by the social worker to connect Mary to meal programs or other formal support services have failed. Except in the coldest temperatures, Mary sleeps on park benches, refusing to stay in the shelters fearing for her safety (on one occasion, she was hit by a younger adult also staying in the shelter). As a result, she is not well known to the shelter staff and receives no structured support in the shelter system.

Assessing Mary's Functional Capacity

The social worker carries out a functional evaluation, assessing Mary's physical, psychological, and social capacity. To evaluate Mary's functional capacity using the capacity–risk model, the social worker answers the capacity indicator questions for the capacity–risk model (see Table 1, chapter 6) to the best of her ability. The results are presented in Table 2.

Table 2: The Capacity–Risk Model: Mary's Capacity Indicators

	Level of capacity		
Physical Capacity: Does the client . . .	High (does regularly without difficulty)	Moderate (does irregularly or with difficulty)	Low (does rarely, with great difficulty, or not at all)
. . . obtain necessary medical care?			×
. . . manage her personal care needs?			×
. . . obtain meals that meet nutritional needs?			×
. . . manage her medications?			×
. . . ambulate and transfer?		×	
Mary's overall physical capacity:			Low

Psychological Capacity: Does the client . . .

	High	Moderate	Low
. . . understand the decisions she is making and their consequences, including the consequences of refusing help?		×	
. . . manage finances and make financial decisions that reflect reasonable judgment?			×
. . . perceive realistically the capacity of informal helpers?		×	
. . . exhibit behavior that is consistent with past lifestyle or an implicit, explicit, or expressed value system?	×		
. . . respond appropriately in emergency and nonroutine situations?		×	
Mary's overall psychological capacity:		Moderate	

continued

The capacity–risk model helps the social worker to view capacity as a multidimensional concept. In contrast to an either–or criterion, the capacity–risk model shows that an individual's capacity can vary along a continuum from low to high. At present, we lack of a quantitative tool to facilitate the synthesis of biopsychosocial data into a numeric measurement that reflects overall functional capacity. Nevertheless, using professional assessment skill and, when available, team consultation, social workers can use the capacity–risk model to conceptualize functional capacity on a continuum from very low to very high. The social worker found Mary's physical capacity to be low, her psychological capacity to be moderate, and her social capacity to be low. Putting this together, the social worker assessed Mary to have low capacity on the capacity axis (see Figure 10).

Table 2: The Capacity–Risk Model: Mary's Capacity Indicators (Continued)

Social Capacity: Does the client have . . .	Level of capacity		
	High (resource available and sufficient to meet client's needs)	Moderate (resource present but inconsistent or not sufficient to meet client's needs)	Low (resource not present)
. . . an informal support system (such as family or friends) that recognizes and responds to the client's needs?		×	
. . . a formal support system (through agencies, providers, or faith communities) that recognizes and responds to the client's needs?			
. . . a living situation and environment that meets the client's basic care needs and is consistent with the client's customary lifestyle?			×
. . . sufficient financial resources to provide for necessities?			×
Mary's overall social capacity:			Low

Mary's Overall Capacity: Type of capacity	Level of capacity		
	High	Moderate	Low
Physical			×
Psychological		×	
Social			×

Assessing Mary's Level of Risk

The next step is for the social worker to evaluate Mary's risk. The capacity–risk model conceptualizes risk from a functional perspective that considers the negative outcomes associated with risks rather than just the presence of risk factors or risk behaviors. Risk is considered unique to each client's circumstances. When evaluating risk, it is important for the social worker to consider the client's values and preferences and how these may affect the client's perception of risk or perception of a negative outcome. A client's psychosocial history can provide insights into his or her risk tolerance level. The social worker should consider any historical data or evidence available to evaluate the client's history for risk tolerance versus risk-aversion decisions.

Figure 10: The Capacity Axis

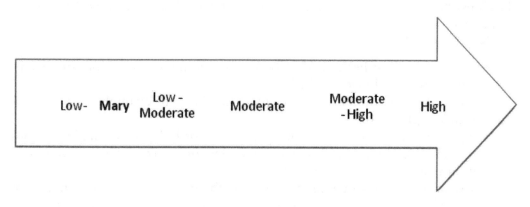

Low-   **Mary**   Low –
Moderate   Moderate   Moderate
-High   High

To assess Mary's risk using the capacity–risk model, the social worker would first consider the "types of risk" Mary faces in the physical, psychological and social arenas.

Physical Risk

The first type of risk within the biopsychosocial framework is physical risk. The capacity–risk model determines physical risk by the "presence of negative conse-quence caused by physical, sensory, or functional limitations" such as the client's inability to carry out an activity of daily living (ADL) or instrumental activity of daily living. To assess Mary's physical risk using the capacity–risk model, the social worker considers the following questions:

Is Mary at risk for

- malnutrition, starvation or dehydration? YES
- hypothermia or hyperthermia? YES
- serious health consequences or physical decline due to untreated or misman-aged medical conditions? YES
- injury due to fire, gas leak, or other hazards caused by functional limita-tions? NO
- serious injury resulting from a fall? YES

With Mary having a total number of four out of five risks present, the social worker identifies her as having a high level of physical risk.

Psychological Risk

The second sphere for risk assessment within the biopsychosocial framework is psy-chological risk. Assessment of psychological risks using the capacity–risk model considers the presence of negative consequences caused by organic, emotional, or behavioral disorders such as dementia, depression, or schizophrenia. To assess Mary's psychological risk using the capacity–risk model, the social worker considers the following questions:

Is Mary at risk for

- disease or serious health decline because of unsanitary conditions (for example, hoarding behaviors)? YES
- physical or emotional trauma from getting lost (for example, as a result of wandering)? NO
- injury or harm resulting from nonpayment of bills (for example, utilities turned off; consequence of unpaid taxes; loss of insurance because of unpaid health, home, or car premiums)? YES
- serious health consequences because of inability to meet needs resulting from mental health issues (for example, depression, obsessive–compulsive disorder)? YES
- psychological or emotional trauma because of mental health problems (for example, emotional trauma from untreated anxiety)? NO
- psychological or emotional trauma because of an inaccurate perception of what is going on in her environment (for example, intense fear caused by delusions or paranoia)? YES

With Mary having a total number of four out of six risks present, the social worker identifies her as having a moderate level of psychological risk.

Social Risk

The third sphere for risk assessment within the biopsychosocial framework is social risk. Using the capacity–risk model, social risk is determined by the presence of negative consequences caused by social, interpersonal, and environmental factors. To assess social risk using the capacity–risk model, the social worker considers the following questions:

Is Mary at risk for

- isolation? NO
- homelessness? YES
- grave injury or death from nonresponse in an emergency? YES
- harm from abuse or neglect by another? YES
- reduction of her financial resources from exploitation or crime? YES
- serious injury resulting from a fall? YES
- destitution (no resources)? YES
- harm caused by unsafe residence, unsound structure, or inoperable utilities? YES
- emotional trauma or cognitive decline resulting from a change in environment (for example, severe depression or confusion after placement in nursing facility)? YES

With Mary having a total number of eight out of nine social risks present, the social worker identifies her as having a high level of social risk.

Overall Risk Assessment

Next, the social worker considers the degree of risk and the degree of certainty that the negative consequences will occur if a situation does not change. Clients like Mary who come to the attention of community-based agencies are frequently experiencing risks from multiple sources. It is often a cumulative effect that changes a situation from one that is manageable or tolerable to one that is considered critical and requires outside intervention. It is essential to understand as completely as possible risks involved in the circumstances of a client who is resistant to accepting help. To determine Mary's overall level of risk, one must consider both types and degrees of risk. Degree of risk can range from high (serious harm, with almost certain probability that a negative event will occur) to moderate or low risk (minimal potential harm, with small probability that a negative event will occur).

The capacity–risk model views risk as a multidimensional concept. At the present time, we lack a quantitative tool to facilitate this synthesis of data into a numeric measurement that reflects overall risk. Nevertheless, using professional assessment skills and, when available, team consultation, social workers can use the capacity–risk model to conceptualize risk on a continuum from very low to very high. The social worker found Mary's physical risk to be high, her psychological risk to be moderate, and her social risk to be high, resulting in an overall high degree of risk. Putting this together, the social worker assessed Mary as having a high risk and marked this on the risk axis (see Figure 11).

Capacity–Risk Model for Assessment of Mary's Overall Level of Functioning

By reflecting on the assessment of the Mary's capacity and the assessment of her level of risk, the social worker is able to conceptualize Mary's functioning as adequate, marginal, or inadequate. This is determined by analyzing the relationship between Mary's capacity and risk.

Mary's capacity is determined to be low, and her risk is determined to be high. The social worker notes the point of intersection of these measures on the capacity–risk graphic tool (see Figure 12). Mary's functional level is inadequate.

Figure 11: The Risk Axis

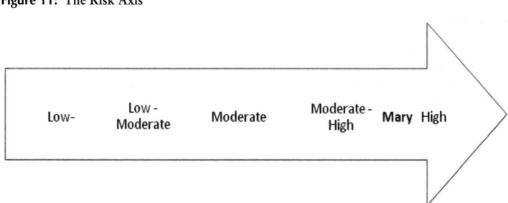

Figure 12: Application of the Capacity–Risk Model to Mary

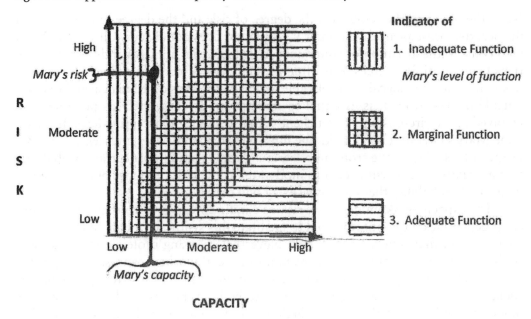

Capacity–Risk Model for Intervention Decisions on Mary

Following assessment, the next question facing the worker is what, if anything, should be done. The social worker uses the capacity–risk model to determine if any level of intervention is appropriate against Mary's wishes. A graphic tool (see Figure 9, p. 85) helps social workers apply the concepts of the capacity–risk model to recommend the appropriate level of intervention.

With low capacity and high risk, the point of intersection on the capacity–risk model indicates that involuntary interventions are appropriate for Mary. These could include petitioning the court for appointment of a guardian. Mary may need a guardian to work toward locating the least restrictive living environment that meets her needs and is as close to her values and preferences as possible.

Summary

For social workers serving vulnerable older adults who refuse interventions, the capacity–risk model offers social workers a framework to apply the social work PIE perspective to the assessment of capacity. In addition to the medical and psychiatric evaluations provided in the hospital.

PART THREE

CHAPTER 9

Working with Older People Who Hoard

Individual and community problems associated with compulsive hoarding have been documented since the late 1940s; however, rigorous, systematic, and empirical studies of hoarding behaviors in older adult populations have only appeared in the literature during the past decade. Compulsive hoarding is a mental health problem that can become a housing, legal, and public health issue in situations that sometimes come to the attention of community social workers who work with older adults. These cases can be very complex and may require social workers to balance difficult decisions about advocating for the rights and best interests of older adult clients, respecting the rights of neighbors and communities, and pursuing protective interventions when necessary to protect vulnerable clients from dangerous and unsafe situations. The capacity–risk model is a useful tool to guide social workers' assessment and intervention decisions when working with older adults who exhibit hoarding behaviors. The model helps social workers to distinguish between situations in which competent and ethical practice require support and respect for a client's right to self-determination and those that require protective interventions. In the following case, Mr. C's attorney referred him for social work assistance.

The client whom we are calling Mr. C is an 84-year-old, never married retiree who lives alone in an apartment he has rented for over 30 years. Maintenance workers who entered Mr. C's apartment to make plumbing repairs expressed concern to his landlord about the condition of his apartment. They reported areas of the kitchen that could not be used because of clutter, blocked passage ways between rooms that were stacked floor to ceiling with boxes, a bathroom tub that was being used as a storage bin, and conditions that they felt were unsafe and created fire hazards for the entire building. Mr. C was served a legal notice to eliminate the clutter and hazards in his apartment within 30 days or risk an eviction notice. Mr. C's landlord suggested to the social worker that at age 84 and with no family to look out for him, it might be better for Mr. C to consider moving into a nursing facility.

Mr. C describes himself as a collector of newspapers, magazines, and other materials which he uses for an ongoing writing project. He also has a large accumulation of small electrical appliances and clocks, which he plans to repair and sell to generate extra income. Mr. C acknowledges that his collecting has gotten out of hand, particularly since pain from arthritis and visual impairments now limits his ability to organize and work on his projects. He wants to remain in his apartment and feels that his landlord is unreasonable to expect him to make drastic changes in the condition of his apartment within 30 days.

Mr. C reports that his medical diagnoses include hypertension and arthritis. He sees his physician about twice a year and has no difficulty managing his medication, getting meals, and managing his finances. He has poor hygiene and personal care, due in part to not having access to his bathtub and having difficulty managing his laundry, house cleaning, and other chores. Mr. C denies past treatment for any psychiatric disorder. He scored in the normal range on a mental status exam and depression screening test. He denies smoking and alcohol use. He reports that he has an older brother who lives in a nursing facility in another state; he has two adult nieces with whom he talks regularly by phone and several close friends who no longer visit because of health problems. He attends church services weekly. Typically, someone from his church checks on him if he misses Sunday services; a church friend also provides biweekly transportation for grocery shopping.

Using the capacity–risk model, the social worker evaluated Mr. C's capacity as high and his risk as moderate. Mr. C agreed to accept social work assistance to work on decreasing or eliminating his hoarding behaviors and to improve the condition of his apartment to comply with his lease requirements for maintaining a safe living environment.

DEFINITION OF HOARDING AND DIAGNOSTIC CRITERIA

Hoarding is a multifaceted problem that involves difficulty with information processing, difficulty with emotional attachments, erroneous beliefs about possessions, and behavioral avoidance. It is characterized by

- the acquisition of, and failure to discard, a large number of possessions that appear to be useless or of limited value;
- living spaces sufficiently cluttered so as to preclude activities for which those spaces were designed; and
- significant distress or impairment in function resulting from the hoarding (Frost & Hartl, 1996).

Hoarding behaviors can coexist with other mental disorders, but they do not always do so. The association between hoarding behavior and obsessive–compulsive disorder (OCD) is not as strong as once thought. Only 17 percent of individuals who have problems with hoarding behaviors are diagnosed with OCD (Tobin, 2007). In one study, community service providers reported that 22 percent of clients who had problems with hoarding behaviors had no other mental health disorder (Steketee, Frost, & Kim, 2001). In the same study, workers reported that the majority of clients (76 percent) had no problems with cognitive functioning or deficits in memory (67 percent). In addition to OCD, hoarding behaviors have been observed in patients with dementia, schizophrenia, major depressive disorder, generalized anxiety disorder, and social phobias.

Until recently, hoarding was studied primarily as a symptom of OCD. However, researchers observed that people with hoarding behaviors often did not meet the diagnostic criteria for OCD and did not respond to the customary treatments for OCD. These customary treatments include medications and cognitive–behavioral therapy (CBT). Observations of differences between the usual presentation of OCD and the clinical presentation of hoarding behaviors led researchers to consider that hoarding behaviors may be diagnostically different from OCD and may warrant a separate designation in the *Diagnostic and Statistical Manual of Mental Disorders* (4th ed., text rev.) (American Psychiatric Association, 2000). These hypotheses led researchers to refine the definition and diagnostic criteria for hoarding, develop measures to describe variations in severity of clutter associated with hoarding behaviors, and test modified approaches to treating adults who have problems with hoarding behaviors.

TREATMENT FOR HOARDING

Two research entities (the Boston University Hoarding Study and the Hartford Hospital Anxiety Disorder Clinic) are testing modified treatment approaches, derived from CBT, that show promise in reducing the symptoms associated with compulsive hoarding and excessive acquiring. Traditional CBT involves 50-minute office sessions. The modified approach involves 26 individual therapy sessions, frequent home visits by clinicians to teach skills in organizing and managing clutter, a room-by-room approach to decluttering, clinician monitoring of progress in the home, homework exercises, exposure to stimuli that may cause fear and anxiety, and help for clients to recognize errors in thinking. The results of the modified CBT approach have shown significant reductions in severity of clutter, difficulty discarding, and acquisition. Clinicians have reported that 50 percent of clients were "much" or "very much" improved with the treatment (Bratiotis, 2008). The treatment model that was described has been published as a guide and manual for mental health therapists (Steketee & Frost, 2007).

Work with individuals who have problems with hoarding behaviors requires longer and more intensive interventions than do traditional therapies; relapse prevention is an essential component of the treatment, and lack of insight and motivation can be significant barriers to treatment.

Adults who have problems with hoarding behaviors can be categorized as those who recognize hoarding behaviors as a problem and seek diagnosis and treatment, those who recognize hoarding behavior as a problem but choose not to seek help, those who experience problems with compulsive hoarding but lack the insight to recognize the behavior and resulting conditions as problematic, and those who have the insight to recognize the behavior and condition as problematic but lack the motivation to address the problem. These differences can be viewed as variations in insight and motivation and can be determining factors in access to treatment and the appropriateness of interventions. Insight and motivation are essential for most psychotherapy interventions. Case management interventions often require professionals to work with clients who lack insight and motivation.

CASE MANAGEMENT

Much of the published research on compulsive hoarding in adults has been conducted with individuals who self-identify as having a problem with hoarding and who volunteer to participate in research studies. These individuals experience distress as a result of their hoarding behavior. In contrast, most of the cases of excessive hoarding that come to the attention of hoarding task forces, adult protective service (APS) agencies, community social workers, home care workers, and court systems consist of individuals who are referred by others. These individuals often deny that hoarding is a problem, may deny that they are distressed by their clutter, and often resist intervention efforts. A study of elder service providers showed that only 15 percent of their clients acknowledged that their hoarding behaviors were irrational; providers reported that 73 percent of their clients had no insight and 12 percent had little insight that their hoarding behavior was irrational or problematic (Steketee et al., 2001).

Working in community settings with adults who may be resistant to accepting help can create ethical and professional challenges for social workers and other professionals who operate within codes of ethics that promote individual autonomy, informed consent, and the right to refuse treatment. It can, in addition, be quite challenging to translate and apply the results from evidence-based practice to work with clients who are resistant to accepting help.

Researchers are developing and testing promising diagnostic criteria and treatment interventions for adults with symptoms of compulsive hoarding. These include neuropsychological studies that are testing psychopharmaceutical interventions (Saxena & Maidment, 2004) and individual and group psychotherapy interventions using a modified form of CBT (Frost, Krause, & Steketee, 1996). These studies have the potential to improve knowledge and practice with adults with compulsive hoarding behaviors who have the insight and motivation to seek treatment. It is also likely that as knowledge and outcomes improve, more people who have problems with compulsive hoarding will seek treatment.

Nevertheless, there will remain a subpopulation of individuals with compulsive hoarding behaviors who only come to the attention of professionals and the public when someone else, usually in a crisis situation, refers them. We live in a society that strongly values individual autonomy, personal freedom, and individual rights. Therefore, professionals have to be careful to avoid paternalistic interventions with adults who have the right and capacity to refuse help and make their own decisions even when these decisions result in poor outcomes. Individuals have varying risk-tolerance levels, and these should be respected. However, there are vulnerable adults who lack the capacity to make their own decisions and who require professional intervention. It is challenging to differentiate between adults in high-risk living situations who are exercising their ethical, civil, and legal rights to make their own choices and those who lack adequate capacity to make informed decisions.

CAPACITY–RISK MODEL

The capacity–risk model is a conceptual framework that guides assessments and intervention decisions in practice with adults who are living in high-risk situations, such as the living conditions of people who struggle with compulsive hoarding. The capacity–risk model applies a biopsychosocial approach that evaluates an individual's ability to function in his or her environment (rather than the more limited assessment of one's ability to process information and make decisions). The model guides practitioners in conducting a comprehensive assessment on physical, psychological, and social functioning that considers the individual's strengths and assets as well as deficits. In the case of Mr. C, we noted that although his hoarding behavior, cluttered apartment, and lack of involved family members represented deficits, his strengths in the areas of physical health, psychological health, and social resources led to an assessment of high to moderate capacity. In this situation, it is appropriate to accept Mr. C's right to make his own decisions about accepting help, despite the risks and potential consequences.

As shown in Figure 8 (see chapter 8, p. 84), the model recognizes that ability to function in one's social environment is not a dichotomous variable, but varies along a continuum (adequate functioning to marginal functioning to inadequate functioning). The model also reflects the reality that in addition to assessing functional capacity, it is also essential to assess the level of risk associated with a person's living situation. Risk is the probability or likelihood that harm or danger will occur if a situation remains unchanged. Like functional capacity, risk is evaluated from a biopsychosocial perspective and varies along a continuum (low risk, moderate risk, high risk). Risk assessment is also a comprehensive evaluation of physical, psychological, and social risks inherent in the client's living situation. Using the capacity–risk model as a guide for assessing adults who do not want to accept services can help community professionals develop skill in recognizing those situations that warrant referrals for protective interventions, namely those cases in which individuals exhibit low capacity and high risk. The model can alternately help practitioners more clearly articulate clinical thinking in situations that require them to accept an individual's right to refuse services.

INTERVENTIONS

One can also use the capacity–risk model to guide intervention decisions when working with older adults whose capacity is assessed as marginal or inadequate. The model helps community workers to recognize that potential interventions with vulnerable adults can vary along a continuum geared toward interventions that enhance capacity, reduce risk, and minimize intrusive and restrictive measures. The case of

Mr. C demonstrated that when a client has high capacity, social workers should respect his or her right to refuse services. When capacity is moderately impaired, social workers can offer be more assertive in efforts to establish a therapeutic alliance with the client, but ultimately, the worker accepts the client's right to refuse services. As noted in chapter 8, use of the capacity–risk model for making decisions about when and how to intervene is based on the following three premises:

Premise 1

When capacity is high, the individual has a right to self-determination regardless of the level of risk present. The professional should accept the individual's right to refuse services.

Premise 2

When capacity is moderate and risk is moderate, professionals should attempt to establish a relationship with the client and client system. If a relationship is established with the client (or client system), the professional should use psychosocial interventions geared toward increasing capacity and decreasing risks. Appropriate interventions include those geared toward relationship development, strengthening the informal social network, enhancing the individual's capacity by providing supportive services, and reducing risk to the individual's health and safety.

Premise 3

When capacity is low and risk is high, professionals have a responsibility to provide protective interventions. These interventions may be involuntary such as referrals to protective service agencies, petitions for guardianship, or evaluations for commitment procedures in situations of imminent danger to self or others. Professionals should pursue interventions that represent the least restrictive alternatives that are most consistent with the client's preferences. Interventions should be geared toward increasing capacity and reducing risk (see Figure 9, chapter 8, p. 85).

The capacity–risk model has been used as a framework for ethical professional practice in protective service agencies, community case management programs, and in home care agencies. Use of the capacity–risk model encourages a systematic approach to assessment and planning interventions with vulnerable older adults. Use of the model can improve community workers' skills in working with vulnerable older adults, as well as empower community workers in their roles as advocates for older adults with impaired capacity and as members of interdisciplinary teams.

CAPACITY-ENHANCEMENT STRATEGIES

Capacity-enhancement and risk-reduction strategies seek to improve the individual's ability to function independently while also decreasing the perceived risks associated with a client's situation. Risk-reduction strategies can guide a social worker in determining how to proceed and incorporate the principles of "least-restrictive alternative" and "maximum client involvement." Capacity-enhancement and risk-reduction principles are fundamental social work problem-solving methods and are listed in Table 3.

The capacity–risk model is derived from established social work practice principles that are conceptualized, focused, and applied in a way that can be used by social workers to structure their thinking about challenging situations and difficult intervention decisions. It does not replace the other tools used in assessing seniors' capacity, function, mental health, and so on, but can be used in conjunction with other tools to guide intervention strategies applied by case managers or hoarding task forces. Both of these intervention strategies are described in the following sections.

The capacity–risk model is an effective conceptual tool to guide assessment and intervention decisions when working with adults who hoard. It is especially useful when working with clients who refuse or resist traditional psychotherapy interventions.

Table 3: Capacity-Enhancement and Risk-Reduction Principles

Capacity Enhancement	Risk Reduction
1. Establish a therapeutic alliance with the client.	1. Identify risk factors.
2. Engage the informal support system in the intervention.	2. Prioritize risk factors, specifying most serious or imminent risk, second most serious or imminent risk, and so on.
3. Identify a "problem for work" that is reflective of something the client wants, even if the client cannot or will not articulate his or her needs.	3. Develop a plan for reducing or eliminating each identified risk factor.
4. Set realistic goals.	4. To the maximum extent possible, involve the client in implementing a plan for risk reduction or eliminating the most serious or imminent risk.
5. Pace interventions to allow adequate time to gain the client's trust.	5. Involve appropriate members of the informal network when the most serious or imminent risk cannot be reduced or eliminated through worker–client interaction.
6. Use informal networks, as appropriate, to enhance the client's capacity.	
7. Use formal services and community resources, as appropriate, to enhance the client's capacity.	6. Involve appropriate formal system when the most serious or imminent risk cannot be reduced or eliminated through worker–client interaction.
8. Continue interventions until the client is no longer at risk.	7. Apply procedures 4 through 6 to reduce or eliminate subsequent risk factors in order of severity, following the resolution of most serious or imminent risk factors.
	8. Continue to implement risk-reduction plans, using strategies outlined in procedures 4 through 6, until all moderate and high risk factors have been eliminated.

CASE MANAGEMENT INTERVENTIONS

There are many reasons why most traditional mental health programs are unable to address the needs of many older adults who have problems with hoarding behaviors, especially those who show limited insight and a lack of motivation to engage in treatment. These reasons include the requirements of therapy (insight and motivation are often essential for initiating therapy), third-party reimbursement requirements (patients have to give authorization to bill their insurance provider for treatment), and limited availability of pro bono and subsidized treatment options. Treatment interventions with adults who hoard are typically long term and intensive, sometimes requiring consultations and interventions by interdisciplinary teams. These are among the reasons why early interventions are the exceptions rather than the rule. Adults who suffer from compulsive hoarding disorders frequently are undiagnosed for many years and may only come to the attention of service providers when their hoarding behaviors generate external pressure from neighbors or community officials or result in crisis situations.

Case management programs often allow for more flexibility in roles (for example, outreach and advocacy) that can be critical in reaching and engaging adults with hoarding behaviors who do not have the insight and motivation that is required for psychotherapy interventions. Skill in establishing therapeutic alliances with clients who may be resistant to accepting help is essential for effective work with this population.

NASW (1992) has described case management as

> a method of providing services whereby a professional social worker assesses the needs of the client and the client's family, when appropriate, and arranges, coordinates, monitors, evaluates, and advocates for a package of multiple services to meet the specific client's complex needs. A professional social worker is the primary provider of social work case management. Distinct from other forms of case management, social work case management addresses both the individual client's biopsychosocial status as well as the state of the social system in which case management operates. Social work case management is both micro and macro in nature: intervention occurs at both the client and the system level. It requires the social worker to develop and maintain a therapeutic relationship with the client, which may include linking the client with systems that provide him or her with needed services, resources, and opportunities.

Social workers often use motivational interviewing and harm-reduction strategies in their case management practice. "Motivational interviewing" evolved from substance abuse treatment methods and was first described by Miller (1983). Motivational interviewing is directive, client-centered counseling style that seeks to bring about behavioral changes by helping clients to explore and resolve ambivalences (Rollnick & Miller, 1995). It differs from confrontational approaches that are often associated with substance abuse therapies by being nonconfrontational and less aggressive. Its primary intent is to increase readiness for change by allowing the client to retain responsibility for problem solving, providing advice and feedback, helping the client to explore options for changing his or her situations, using an empathetic counseling style, and using a strengths and empowerment perspective (Rollnick & Miller, 1995). Using motivational interviewing strategies is a more directive method than traditional therapies and less confrontational than traditional substance abuse treatment methods.

"Harm-reduction therapy" is also derived from substance abuse treatment methods. It is a nonjudgmental approach that seeks to reduce the negative effect of hoarding. Harm-reduction therapy recognizes that hoarding behaviors and problems exist for a reason and satisfy needs of the individual that may not be apparent to the practitioner. Harm-reduction therapy is based on the principals of collaboration, respect, and self-determination (Harm Reduction Psychotherapy and Training Associates, n.d.).

OTHER EMERGING INTERVENTIONS

Professional Organizers

As compulsive hoarding gains increasing recognition as a problem, new industries and professions are emerging in the private sector to address the environmental conditions that can result from compulsive hoarding behaviors. Private services include professional organizers, decluttering, heavy-duty cleaning services, and move managers. National groups have emerged to respond to growing awareness of problems associated with clutter, disorganization, and hoarding. The National Association of Professional Organizers (NAPO) was established in 1985 and currently has 34 chapters throughout the United States (see http://www.napo.net/). NAPO offers education and certification for professional organizers. The National Study Group on Chronic Disorganization also offers education and certification for professional organizers (see http://www.nsgcd.org/).

Heavy-Duty Cleaning Services

In Washington, DC, and other jurisdictions, limited governmental funding has been allocated for "heavy-duty cleaning programs" as an adjunct to professional interventions in hoarding cases. These services are usually provided through APS programs, nonprofit home care agencies, and other community social service programs. Across the country, commercial, fee-for-service programs are being marketed to address hoarding problems. Landlords and family member sometimes engage these services in response to the threat of eviction for lease violations and unsafe and unsanitary housing situations. There is a growing consensus that heavy-duty cleaning services are not effective as a long-term solution to problems with hoarding behavior. Unless other, continuing, long-term services are implemented, the hoarding and clutter conditions will recur. In Washington, DC, older people with hoarding problems sometime agree to heavy-duty cleaning when threatened with eviction. These services can avert a pending eviction but often result in emotional trauma for the older adult, and they can have a negative effect on relationships between the older person and the professionals who help to arrange the service.

Volunteer Services

Communities across the country are beginning to recruit and train special volunteers to work with individuals who have problems with hoarding. Washington, D.C. is home to the Elder Buddies Program, an intergenerational volunteer program that addresses the needs of older people and people with disabilities who are at risk for eviction. The Elder Buddies Program is part of AARP's Legal Counsel for the Elderly's Alternatives to Landlord/Tenant Court for the Elderly Project ("Alternatives Project"), which began in 1999 to protect elders from the trauma of eviction (AARP, 2007). The Alternatives Project consists of an attorney supervisor, a part-time licensed clinical social worker, and an Elder Buddies volunteer who provides the housekeeping and decluttering help clients need to remain living independently in their own apartments (AARP, 2007). Elder Buddies provides community service opportunities for high school and college students and young adult volunteers. Elder buddies work in small groups, with adult supervision, and often form meaningful, short-term relationships with older people that are mutually life enhancing. The DC Elder Buddies program recruits, trains, and supervises more than 360 young volunteers a year and has prevented evictions for more than 200 elders (some with serious hoarding problems). The program estimates that it saves tenants, Washington, DC, government, and private landlords $70 thousand annually in legal fees and the cost for cleaning services. The following blog post, from an Elder Buddy, illustrates the multiple values derived through this program:

> When considering homelessness, I never really think about the prevention side of things. Elder Buddies, an organization under Faith in Action and the AARP (I believe), does wonders for the elderly in homeless prevention.
>
> I recently volunteered with this org[anization]. My group was assigned to a hoarder. She was in her 30 day grace period because management had already issued her an eviction notice. When we walked into her apartment it was knee high/thigh high with stuff. At the end of the first day we had emptied out about 3½ dumpsters of things she was hoarding. And that was just the living room and walk through hallway! There was so much more to go but the woman, who was definitely having doubts when our crew walked in, was so excited to be able to sit on her living room couch at the end of the day. People have asked me if she was having mental issues, but she wasn't. She was actually very aware. She had traveled all over the world and just let her "collection" of stuff get out of hand. Looking at her, was like a glimpse into my future. I keep a LOT of stuff . . . for memory's sake or in case I'll "need" something in the future. I can see myself getting to her age and wanting keepsakes from all my life's travels. Plus if I was living by myself . . . all my hoarded stuff would help fill the space and I might not feel as lonely.

If we hadn't started to clean out this woman's apartment, she would have ended up homeless. Either from a fire (SERIOUS fire hazard) or because she would have been kicked out by management. (F., 2008)

HOARDING TASK FORCES

Across the country, an interesting community-level approach has evolved for furthering interdisciplinary understanding of hoarding, educating professionals and consumers about hoarding, and formulating community specific policies and protocols to address problems that come to the attention of public health, mental health, and social service agencies. Some hoarding task forces are headed and directed by public agencies with a community focus, such as housing and code departments, fire and rescue departments or code enforcement departments of local or county governments. Others are formed and directed by social service and mental health agencies, such as academic gerontology programs, state and local aging departments, APS agencies, or county mental health programs. Some task forces are deliberately formed as short-term forums for community collaboration; others function as ongoing programs that accept referrals and engage professionals from different agencies in a process of "case sharing." In most instances, hoarding task forces represent community efforts to achieve a balance between respect for the rights of individuals who have problems with hoarding behavior, while also recognizing the rights of neighbors and the need to enforce community standards for public health and safety. Most task forces are voluntary and unfunded; however, some have been incorporated into the community infrastructure through legislation and designated funding.

IMPLICATIONS

Community work with individuals with hoarding behaviors who are resistant to accepting help has the potential to increase the individual's ability to achieve his or her preferred outcomes and prevents evictions, homelessness, and institutional placement. For vulnerable adults, successful interventions are those that include outreach, assessment of capacity, assessment of risks, and interventions that are geared toward increasing capacity and reducing harm and risk. These interventions may be psychosocial or may involve initiating processes for legal protections, such as guardianship or conservatorship.

The capacity–risk model can be a tool used by a range of community workers working with adults who struggle with hoarding, including examiners or evaluators who are preparing a report for the court in guardianship hearings of vulnerable older adults. The judicial determination of competence is largely dependent on the information included in the clinical assessment. There is currently great variability in the role and scope and format of clinical capacity assessments used to guide the judicial determination of capacity and its effect on guardianship (Moye, Wood, et al., 2007). A standard set of areas to be included in assessment is being recommended for all guardianship cases of older adults. Physicians and psychologists traditionally have been asked to provide the information used in the examiners' reports. With the recognition that a broader, more standard area of information is needed, the courts have also become more accepting of nonphysicians as experts who can provide evidence about capacities (Zarit & Zarit, 2007). The field of social work is well trained and suited as a profession to offer its expertise as examiners in guardianship cases. In situations in which the older adult is at risk and resistant to accepting help, the capacity–risk model can guide social workers with recommendations regarding capacity, risk, and the need for the court to intervene against the will of the older adult.

CHAPTER 10

Live Alones: Social Work Interventions with People with Alzheimer's Disease and Related Dementias Who Live Alone

Patients with dementia who live alone represent a very significant, yet unstudied, segment of the Alzheimer's disease and related dementias (ADRD) population. Although this population is relatively small, these individuals are frequently very vulnerable and have a greater than usual need for outreach, community support, and health and social services. Most have family members who are involved in their care. However, within the ADRD population that lives alone, there are "elderly orphans" who rely on distant kin, friends, neighbors, and other nontraditional caregivers. These nontraditional caregivers of dementia patients often don't know where to turn for information, education, support, and assistance in carrying out their caregiver roles. Some ADRD patients have no one to assume a caregiver role. We know very little about the profile, support systems, and needs of dementia patients who live alone, especially those without close kin.

Most of what we know about caregiving for people with ADRD derives from studies of family caregivers. Many participants in research studies are referred or encouraged to participate by family members. Research sampling procedures often eliminate patients who do not have family caregivers. Obtaining informed consent to participate in research studies can be difficult when there is no family member to serve as a surrogate decision maker. Findings from ADRD caregiving studies consequently focus on family caregivers. The assumptions have been that few patients with dementia live alone, and that support and involvement from family caregivers is an essential component of managing the illness.

Increasingly, we are recognizing that these assumptions are not correct. Social workers are seeing more and more people with moderate to severe dementia who are living alone, including some who have no informal caregiver.

This chapter summarizes what we know about people with ADRD who live alone. We present information from published and unpublished studies about the number and types of people with dementia who live alone, their characteristics, and common problems that arise in working with them. We also discuss goals that social work agencies might consider in creating a community system to meet the needs of this segment of the ADRD population.

HOW MANY PEOPLE WITH ADRD LIVE ALONE?

Precise numbers are not available. It was thought until recently that very few people with dementia live alone. The few studies that identified ADRD patients who lived alone suggested that they were only mildly impaired (Congressional Office of Technological Assessment [COTA], 1990). Living alone with dementia was thought to occur only in the early stages of the illness. However, estimates drawn from population surveys of dementia patients suggest that at least 20 percent of people with dementia live alone (Ginther & Fox, 1991; Webber, Fox, & Burnette, 1994). It is estimated that half do not have family caregivers. At least some of these have severe cognitive impairments (COTA, 1990). A California study estimates that 10 percent of all people with dementia live alone and have no caregiver (COTA, 1990).

Patients with dementia who live alone are largely a hidden population, frequently not coming to the attention of researchers (Soniat & Pollack, 1992). Much of what we know is from anecdotal accounts from workers in community service programs (gatekeeper programs, adult protective services [APS], home care programs, community based case managers, court systems). The limited studies that have been conducted are based on small, nonrandom samples (Ginther & Fox, 1991; Soniat & Pollack, 1992, 1993a; Webber et al., 1994), thus, the findings cannot be generalized across communities.

The overall numbers are relatively small because the illness itself affects a minority of older people. It is estimated that ADRD affects 5 to 10 percent of the population that is over 65 years old. The incidence of the illness increases to 47 percent for those over 85. For live alones, diagnosis of the illness may be delayed, especially when there is no family caregiver to encourage medical evaluation of changes in an individual's behaviors and cognitive abilities. Thus, this population frequently comes to the attention of health professionals and service providers later in their illness, often in response to crisis situations.

Targeting patients with dementia who live alone, especially those without caregivers, is similar to finding and treating rare diseases. The number of people afflicted is relatively small; however the impact of the illness and implications for treatment and care are tremendous. We lack screening devices for early identification of ADRD live alones. Dementia patients who live alone without support from family caregivers are the most vulnerable ADRD patient population. Locating them and providing the care and help they need is a special challenge to communities across the country.

WHO ARE THE PEOPLE WITH ADRD WHO LIVE ALONE AND WHERE DO THEY LIVE?

There is no comprehensive information that describes ADRD patients who live alone. For historical and sociological reasons, certain kinds of elderly people who live alone tend to be in particular areas and communities. For example, the following reports describe ADRD populations identified by Alzheimer's Association chapters and others across the states (see http://www.alz.org/index.asp):

- older people in rural areas whose spouses have died and whose children have moved away;
- elderly women who came to Washington, DC, 50 or more years ago to work for the federal government during the war, never married or had children, and now live alone;
- elderly Chinese men who came to California to work on the railroad, never married or had children, and now live alone;
- elderly men who went to Alaska to look for gold, never married or had children, and now live alone; and
- older people who moved to Florida with a spouse who subsequently died (these individuals frequently have children in other states who may not be immediately aware of the needs of the remaining parent).

Because of these differences in gender, culture, socioeconomic status, and community history, efforts to create a community system to meet the needs of people with ADRD who live alone must be community specific. The effort must begin at individual community levels to determine who they are and where they live. It is estimated that, overall, 30 percent of noninstitutionalized older people live alone (U.S. Department of Health and Human Services, Administration on Aging, 2008). Thirty-one states and Washington, DC, have higher than average populations of older people who live alone. For some states, analyses of migration and population trends shed some light on why there are larger than average numbers of older people who live alone. Yet, even in those states with live-alone populations less than the national average, Alzheimer's Association chapters report communities in which significant numbers of ADRD patients live alone.

The Washington, DC, Office on Aging, in collaboration with the Alzheimer's Association, has supported the development of a number of services that support ADRD patients who live alone. In this chapter, we discuss some of these initiatives that might be replicated in other jurisdictions.

CATEGORIES OF PEOPLE WITH ADRD WHO LIVE ALONE

Three categories of people with dementia who live alone have been identified (Soniat & Pollock, 1993a):

- The most typical are ADRD patients who live alone but receive frequent monitoring and support from close kin who live nearby.

- The second most typical are ADRD patients who live alone with support from long-distance caregivers, usually adult children or siblings.
- The most vulnerable are ADRD patients who live alone and have no identifiable close-kin relationships.

Among the latter population of ADRD patients, there are those who have distant kin relatives (nephew, nieces, or cousins) who live in the area, those who have distant kin who live out of town, and "elderly orphans"—ADRD patients with no identifiable kin relationships. "Elderly orphans" with ADRD are the least typical and eventually become known to APS agencies and court systems that handle guardianship and conservatorship cases. Earlier identification of this population is critical for preventing neglect of medical care, personal care, and financial management needs, and for reducing the risks for fraud, financial exploitation, and unsafe living conditions.

The options for care differ, based on the three categories listed above. Special initiatives are needed to serve each group. Most of what we know about caregiving for ADRD patients concerns caregiving by spouses, adult children, and, to a lesser extent, siblings. Little is known about the roles that more distant kin (nieces, nephews, cousins) play when ADRD patients live alone and do not have a spouse, child, or sibling. These more distant relatives are frequently uncomfortable assuming responsibility for ADRD patients and often lack knowledge and information on how to carry out their "next of kin" role. Some have not had consistent, long-term relationships with the person, and are unaware of their history, values, and preferences. When patients lack even distant kin, friends and neighbors are at an even greater disadvantage in knowing how to help and where to turn for assistance. There are frequently unclear guidelines on who can make healthcare and other decisions when an ADRD patient has no close kin.

LITERATURE REVIEW AND THEORETICAL BACKGROUND

Shanas (1979) and Cantor (1975) conducted research that established the principles of hierarchical compensation and substitution models for informal caregiving. These principles suggest that the choice of caregiver follows a hierarchical pattern. The choice of caregiver is usually a spouse. When a spouse is not available, an adult daughter usually serves as primary caregiver. When there is neither a spouse nor adult daughter, another relative assumes major caregiving responsibilities. When no family members are available to provide care, older people turn to neighbors, friends, and eventually formal organizations (Cantor & Little, 1985).

For a variety of reasons, research on informal supports has focused primarily on the family rather than friends, neighbors, and formal organizations (Cantor & Little, 1985). Friends and neighbors are thought to be of particular importance in the lives of the well and mildly impaired elderly (Cantor & Little, 1985; Lawton, Brody & Turner-Massey, 1978).

A few studies have looked at the role of siblings in the lives of widowed, childless, and never-married elderly (Cantor, 1991; Johnson & Catalano, 1981; Shanas, 1979). These studies show that, in some instances, siblings take on the characteristics of an elderly spouse caregiver. These characteristics include extensive time involvement, performance of many kinds of tasks, and experiencing intense emotional and physical strain in the caregiving role. Less is known about the roles performed by more distant kin and nonfamily caregivers.

The support system literature includes a few anecdotal references to "fictive kin," people who assume familylike functions in the lives of people who do not have traditional family relationships (Greene & Soniat, 1991; Streib, 1977). This phenomenon has not been examined empirically for any population, but may be found to function within the networks of older people with dementia who live alone. The few reported studies of older people without family (C. Cohen & Rajkowski, 1982; Johnson & Catalano, 1981) suggest that friend and neighbor networks act in a compensatory manner, assuming many of the functions of family when family members are absent from the support system.

A number of exploratory studies have been conducted with samples from the Washington, DC, ADRD live-alone population. A 1990 geriatric clinic and case management site chart review (see Soniat & Pollack, 1992) identified 54 cognitively impaired patients who had been admitted to the programs within the preceding year. All lived alone and did not have a family caregiver. Follow-up on these cases, four months later, found that one-third were no longer living alone in the community. Eleven were in nursing homes, four had moved into assisted-living arrangements, and three had died. This study demonstrated the dynamic changes that occurred within the sample over a relatively short period of time (four months).

The follow-up data were obtained from chart reviews and unstructured interviews with case managers. Some of the unanswered questions from this case review were the following: What factors influenced these outcomes? What were the specific caregiving arrangements associated with different outcomes? Were there differences in severity of illness associated with the different outcomes? How were the decisions made for nursing home placements and moves to assisted housing?

In October 1993, Soniat and Pollack (1993b) completed a retrospective review of 61 closed cases of patients with ADRD living alone who had received services from two case management sites (George Washington University and IONA Senior Services) between October 1990 and September 1993. The sample was evenly divided between those who had an identified family member ($n = 31$) and those with no kin relationships (orphans) ($n = 31$). The mean age of the sample was 85 years. Of those reviewed, 89 percent were female. The sample was 90 percent white. There were differences between orphans and those with family on measures of marital status, length of case management services, primary decision maker, and outcomes (that is, why the case was closed).

Orphans were equally as likely to have been never married (49 percent) or widowed (49 percent). ADRD patients who lived alone but had family were more likely to have been widowed (61 percent). Within the population overall, only 4 to 5 percent of older people were never married. Thus, people who were never married are at very high risk for needing and not having a caregiver in old age. This factor may help in providing guideline on how to find ADRD patients who live alone, and how to target preventive interventions such as advanced planning for long-term care initiatives.

The average length of case management services was 20.96 months for orphans, compared with 14.7 months for those with family. The measurable outcomes noted at the time of closure were living at home with no further need for case management services (18 percent), moved to assisted living facility (15 percent), moved to nursing home (45 percent), and deceased (22 percent). These outcomes differed for orphans and those with family.

Orphans were equally as likely to have died while living in the community and still needing case management services (39 percent) or to have moved to a nursing home (39 percent). Those with family were more likely to have moved to a nursing home (59 percent), assisted living facility (19 percent), or remained at home with no further need for case management services (16 percent). Six percent of those who had family moved in with a family member. Only three (10 percent) of those with family died while living in the community and needing case management services at the time of their death.

Overall, 5 percent of the sample had no one identified as a surrogate decision maker. Family members were surrogate decision makers in 40 percent of the cases. Attorneys were surrogate decision makers for 25 percent of the sample. These included voluntary legal arrangements and court-appointed guardians and conservators. In 30 percent of the cases, people without clear familial, voluntarily granted, or legal authority made surrogate decisions. These included friends and neighbors (14 percent) and others (that is, doctors, case managers, hospital discharge planners, and resident managers of apartment buildings) (16 percent).

As expected, surrogate decision makers differed by family type. For those with identified family, including close and distant kin, a family member made surrogate decisions in 77 percent of the cases. Surrogate decision making, without clear authority, occurred for 48 percent of the orphans. This was the most prevalent form of decision making for orphans. Only 16 percent of those who had family had decisions made by people without clear familial, voluntarily granted, or legal authority. Only 7 percent of those with family had legal decision makers. Of orphans, 42 percent had legal decision makers.

These preliminary data firmly established the need for a more systematic study of individuals with ADRD who live alone. The findings from the retrospective chart review were based on existing data that was not collected for research purposes. For example, from the preliminary data, we were unable to determine systematically the extent to which advanced directives, powers of attorney, trust agreements, court procedures, and informal verbal agreements were used to direct decision-making.

The two case management sites that provided preliminary data for the just-discussed study were atypical for Washington, DC, and represented a geographic area that was predominantly white and with a higher socioeconomic status. Income and education are factors that influence care options and, perhaps, the probability that individuals will plan in advance for long-term care needs.

A more systematic pilot study (Soniat & Pollack, 1996) focused on the community dwelling cognitively impaired without family caregivers (elderly orphans). It further demonstrated that nonfamily informal support networks supported the ADRD live-alone population. These networks varied in composition and roles assumed and differed in structure from networks typically reported in the literature on caregivers of ADRD patients. Specifically these networks consisted of sibling, more distant kin (that is, nieces, nephews, or cousins) and nonkin relationships (that is, friends, neighbors, or apartment managers). The data suggested that these networks were often of long-term duration, involved strong bonds of affection and commitment, contributed significant resources in time and tasks, and functioned to sustain patients in the community for long periods following the appearance of symptoms of ADRD.

A nonmedical crisis—related to cognitive deficits, behavioral symptoms, or caregiving concerns—most often brought cases to the attention of the healthcare and community service systems (relocation or vacation plans of a very involved neighbor, small fires or smoke from unattended cooking utensils, wandering that required the filing of missing persons reports, or crises created by lost keys). Differences in the composition and roles assumed by the nonfamily informal networks influenced decision making, home care service use, and need for nursing home care. Networks that included relationships that were long term were least likely to require court interventions. Few used community services, in part because it was difficult to arrange or obtain acceptance and cooperation from the patient. The study was cross-sectional, so longitudinal data are not available; however, in general, very few nonfamily caregivers had anticipated the progressive nature of the disease and how future needs of the patients would be addressed.

One of the few published studies of ADRD patients who live alone (Webber et al., 1994) focused on use of formal services by this population. The researchers found that ADRD patients who lived alone were significantly different from ADRD patients who lived with others. ADRD patients living alone were found to be older, poorer, and less impaired than those living with others. Of these, 30 percent did not have an identified caregiver. Living alone was a significant predictor of no service use. When ADRD patients living alone used services, they were more likely to use case management services, home delivered meals, and homemaker or chore services. They were less likely to use physician services, hospital services, and adult day care services. An unexpected finding was that living alone reduced the odds for nursing home placement. Although the researchers attributed this finding to probable sample bias, it is likely that factors related to the availability of a surrogate decision maker play a significant role in determining outcomes and placement options for ADRD patients who live alone.

Although the progressive nature of ADRD predicates that someone other than the patient has to eventually become involved in making care decisions, there are no studies that specifically address this issue. Understanding the processes and mechanisms for decision making when ADRD patients live alone is critical, particularly when there are no family caregivers.

WHAT DO WE KNOW ABOUT THE CHARACTERISTICS, PROBLEMS, AND SERVICE NEEDS OF PEOPLE WITH ADRD WHO LIVE ALONE?

Much of what is known about dementia patients who live alone comes from small community samples and anecdotal accounts of professionals who work in communities (home care workers, APS workers, and case managers). The lack of systematic data highlight the need to develop strategies for projecting the size of the population, implementing outreach and early case finding approaches, conducting longitudinal studies, and disseminating practice data and effective program models across jurisdictions. The following summarizes what is currently known about ADRD patients who live alone.

Severity of Dementia

Although it is generally assumed that people with dementia who live alone have only mild cognitive impairments, research shows that is not true. In fact, significant numbers of people with moderate and severe dementia also live alone. Anecdotal evidence indicates that people with moderate or severe dementia who live alone tend to be in the third category—that is, they have no informal caregiver.

Financial Status

Some people with dementia who live alone have significant or adequate income and assets, and others do not. It should not be assumed that they are all poor.

Functional Limitations

We have no comprehensive information, but some studies indicate that people with dementia who live alone are more likely to have limitations in instrumental activities of daily living, especially limitations in ability to manage their own money than in activities of daily living.

Connection to Healthcare and Social Service Providers

People with dementia who live alone and have no informal caregiver are likely to drop out of the healthcare system. No one reminds them to make physician appointments, and they cannot remember to do so. They are likely to come to the attention of healthcare and social service providers at a time of crisis.

Likelihood of Nursing Home Placement

People with dementia who live alone and have no informal caregiver may be less likely than those who have a caregiver to be placed in a nursing home because no one is aware of their condition and care needs. People with dementia who live alone and have an informal caregiver, especially a long-distance caregiver, may be more likely to be placed in a nursing home because the informal caregiver is anxious about their safety.

Vulnerability to Fraud

People with dementia who live alone are vulnerable to fraud, including financial scams by individuals who intend to take advantage of them and situations in which someone who has good intentions (for example, a neighbor or home health aide) provides important assistance over time but eventually steals from them.

Service Needs

People with dementia who live alone and have no family caregiver need many of the same kinds of help as those who live with someone or have a family caregiver. Two special needs are: (1) the need for help in managing money and (2) the need for help with decision making.

Guardianship and Power of Attorney

Most people with dementia, including those who live alone and have no informal caregiver, do not have a legal guardian or power of attorney. In many communities, it is difficult, if not impossible, to find someone to act as a legal guardian, especially for a person who does not have substantial income and assets.

WHAT GOALS SHOULD WE HAVE IN WORKING WITH PEOPLE WITH ADRD WHO LIVE ALONE?

We assume, intuitively, that ADRD patients who live alone, and particularly those without family caregivers, are best cared for in assisted living facilities or institutional settings. However, when we examine the actual experiences of ADRD patients who live alone, we find that many live in their own homes and communities for many years before coming to the attention of professional service providers. With support from nontraditional care givers and communities, a variety of community-based care options are available to ADRD patients who live alone. Many live most or all of their illness in their own home. This suggests that we may be able to learn more about living with ADRD by objectively examining this population and its informal care arrangements.

The following are recommended goals to guide policies and program planning for ADRD patients who live alone:

- Provide support to maintain as much independence as possible.
- Identify specific risks of living alone with ADRD and programs to minimize risk factors.
- Anticipate and plan to avoid crisis situations.
- Avoid global, generalized interventions that do not take into account the unique needs and resources of individual communities and patient care systems.

WHAT IS NEEDED IN A COMMUNITY SYSTEM TO MEET THE NEEDS OF PEOPLE WITH ADRD WHO LIVE ALONE?

Four types of programs supported by the Washington, DC, Office on Aging suggest specialized approaches that communities might consider to address the needs of the ADRD population. These include "geriatric case management" programs that are available on the basis of need (rather than income or third-party reimbursement requirements) and that target outreach and service efforts toward ADRD patients who live alone; Al-Care, a specialized homemaker service program for ADRD patients; "Stand in the Gap," a research and demonstration project to monitor the needs of the population, achieve community collaboration, and to develop specialized programs in response to identified needs; and the Protective Arrangement and Evaluation Panel, an interdisciplinary consultation and advisory panel that brings together attorneys, social workers, community nurses, and an ethics specialist to hear cases on a regular basis and recommend safe, least-restrictive alternatives for protection and care.

Al-Care developed a manual to provide a model for home care services for dementia patients, including those who live alone. Many home care agencies refuse to provide services to ADRD patients who do not have involved family caregivers, based on the assumption that by doing so, they are perpetuating an unsafe situation. Others are concerned that providing the service is not cost effective; patients sometimes have difficulty developing new relationships and may not readily recognize or admit the home care worker. Agencies also fear liabilities, especially when workers are falsely accused of taking possessions that the patients may have misplaced. Al-Care's experiences in working with this population, including selecting and training specialized home care providers, may encourage other communities to provide incentives to agencies to develop similar programs.

Other communities have developed "gatekeeper" programs to involve postal workers, meter readers, newspaper carriers, and others in an effort to monitor the needs of vulnerable community residents. Gatekeeper programs are virtually cost-free programs that have been effectively adopted in many communities.

In general, community efforts are needed to develop policies and programs that address the following:

- ways to identify the population;
- programs that recognize the special problems that arise in working with ADRD live alones, including difficult issues in decision making for people with questionable or fluctuating decision-making capacity;
- the need for joint planning and involvement of a wide array of healthcare and social service providers and others in the community who come in contact with and may help to identify and care for them, including pastors, rabbis, lawyers, mail carriers, and so forth; and
- training and supports for healthcare and social service providers who work with them, including home care workers and case managers.

CONCLUSIONS

To achieve these goals, it is important to establish a community system for identifying and meeting the needs of people with ADRD who live alone. Those without family caregivers are particularly vulnerable. It is only within recent years that communities have begun to recognize the existence and needs of this population. Thus, the service needs of the population overall has been given little attention. Family and nonfamily caregivers of ADRD patients who live alone have specialized needs for information, support, and assistance. The social work profession is in a unique position to be proactive in planning interventions, particularly preventive interventions, to reduce the vulnerability of ADRD patients who live alone, particularly those without close kin. The capacity–risk model can be an important educational and assessment tool to inform social work practice with this vulnerable group of older adults.

References

AARP. (2007, January 5). *Alternatives to Landlord/Tenant Court for the Elderly Project*. Retrieved from http://cq5.share.aarp.org/makeadifference/gettinghelp/articles/elder_buddies.html

Abramson, M. (1985). The autonomy–paternalism dilemma in social work practice. *Social Casework, 66,* 387–393.

Adams, J. (1996). Self-neglect in later life. *Health and Social Care in the Community, 4,* 226–233.

Altman, W. M., Parmelee, P. A., & Smyer, M. A. (1992). Autonomy, competence, and informed consent in long term care: Legal and psychological perspectives. *Villanova Law Review, 37,* 1671–1704.

American Bar Association & American Psychological Association. (2005). *Assessment of older adults with diminished capacity: A handbook for lawyers*. Washington, DC: Author.

American Bar Association & American Psychological Association. (2008). *Assessment of older adults with diminished capacity: A handbook for psychologists*. Washington, DC: Author.

American Bar Association, American Psychological Association, & National College of Probate Judges. (2006). *Judicial determination of capacity of older adults in guardianship proceedings*. Washington, DC: Author.

American Psychiatric Association. (2000). *Diagnostic and statistical manual of mental disorders* (4th ed., text rev.). Washington, DC: Author.

Angel, R. J., & Frisco, M. L. (2001). Self-assessments of health and functional capacity among older adults. *Journal of Mental Health and Aging, 7,* 119–138.

Appelbaum, P. S. (2007). Assessment of patient's competence to consent to treatment. *New England Journal of Medicine, 357,* 1834–1840.

Appelbaum, P. S., & Grisso, T. (1988). Assessing patient's capacities to consent to treatment. *New England Journal of Medicine, 319,* 1635–1638.

Association of American Physicians and Surgeons. (n.d.). *How to opt out of Medicare*. Retrieved from http://www.aapsonline.org/medicare/optout.htm

Barker, R. L. (2003). *The social work dictionary* (5th ed.). Washington, DC: NASW Press.

Berg-Weger, M. (2005). *Social work and social welfare: An invitation*. Boston: McGraw-Hill.

Bond, J., & Corner, L. (2004). *Quality of life and older people*. Buckingham, England: Open University Press.

Bordin, E. S. (1979). The generalizability of the psychoanalytic concept of the working alliance. *Psychotherapy: Theory, Research, & Practice, 16,* 252–260.

Bratiotis, C. (2008, June 26). Keynote address at the National Catholic School of Social Service Community Forum on Hoarding, Catholic University of America, Washington, DC.

Brearley, C. P. (1982). *Risk and social work: Hazards and helping*. London: Routledge & Kegan Paul.

Butler, R., & Lewis, M., (1982). *Aging and mental health: Positive psychosocial and biomedical approaches* (3rd ed). Boston: Allyn & Bacon.

Cantor M. H. (1975). Life space and the social support system of the inner city elderly of New York. *Gerontologist, 15,* 23–27.

Cantor M. H. (1991). Family and community: Changing roles in an aging society. *Gerontologist, 31,* 337–346.

Cantor, M.,& Little, V. (1985). Aging and social care. In R. H. Binstock & E. Shanas (Eds.), *Handbook of aging and the social sciences* (pp. 745–781). New York: Van Nostrand Reinhold.

Checkland, D., & Silberfeld, M. (1993). Competence and the three A's: Autonomy, authenticity, and aging. *Canadian Journal of Aging, 12,* 454–468.

Cohen, C., & Rajkowski, H. (1982). What's in a friend? Substantive and theoretical issues. *Gerontologist, 22,* 261–266.

Cohen, G. D. (1994). The geriatric landscape: Toward a health and humanities research agenda in aging. *American Journal of Geriatric Psychiatry, 2,* 185–187.

Compton, B., & Galaway, B. (1989). *Social work processes* (4th ed.) Belmont, CA: Wadsworth.

Compton, B., & Galaway, B. (1994). *Social work processes* (5th ed.). Pacific Grove, CA: Brooks/Cole.

Congressional Office of Technological Assessment. (1990). *Confused minds, burdened families: Finding help for people with Alzheimer's disease and other dementias* (Publication No. OTA-BA-403). Washington, DC: U.S. Government Printing Office.

Conrad, A. P. & Joseph, M. V. (2006). A code for our times. *Catholic Charities USA, 33,* 32–33.

Coren, S., Ward, L. M., & Enns, J. T. (1999). *Sensation and perception* (5th ed.). Fort Worth, TX: Harcourt Brace College.

Council on Social Work Education. (n.d.). *National Center for Gerontological Social Work Education.* Retrieved from http://www.cswe.org

Council on Social Work Education. (2009). *Advanced gero social work practice.* Retrieved from http://www.cswe.org

County of Los Angeles Community and Senior Services. (2005). *APS client/risk assessment (CSS/APS-RA1).* Retrieved from http://css.lacounty.gov/Bid/docs/APS/exhibit_D/APS%20RA1%20%20APS%20Client%20RiskAssessment.pdf

Cowger, C.D. (1992). Assessment of client strengths. In D. Saleebey (Ed.), *The strengths perspective in social work practice* (pp. 139–147). New York: Longman.

Davis, M. (1992). Client's right to self determination. *Caring, 11,* 26–32.

Duke University Center for the Study of Aging and Human Development. (1978). *Multidimensional functional assessment: The OARSS methodology.* Durham, NC: Author.

Engel, G. L. (1978). Biopsychosocial model and the education of health professionals. In C. D. Burrell (Ed.), *Primary health care in industrialized nations: Annals of the New York Academy of Sciences* (Volume 310, pp. 169–181). New York: New York Academy of Sciences.

Ferri, C. P., Prince, M., Brayne, C., Brodaty, H., Fratiglioni, L., Ganguli, M., et al. (2005). Global prevalence of dementia: A Delphi consensus study. *Lancet, 366,* 2112–2117.

Folstein, M. F., Folstein, S., & McHugh, P. R. (1975). Mini-mental state: A practical method for grading the cognitive state of patients for the clinician. *Journal of Psychiatric Research, 12,* 189–198.

Frost, R., & Hartl, T. L. (1996). A cognitive–behavioral model of compulsive hoarding. *Behavior Research and Therapy, 34,* 341–350.

Frost, R., Krause, M., & Steketee, G. (1996). Hoarding and obsessive–compulsive symptoms. *Behavior Modification, 20,* 116–132.

F. T. (2008, March 24). Elder Buddies. Review posted to http://www.yelp.com/biz/elder-buddies-washington

Galantowicz, S., & Selig, B. (2005, February 15). *Risk management and quality in HCBC: Individual risk planning and prevention, system-wide quality improvement.* Retrieved from http://www.hcbs.org/files/60/2986/Risk_Management_and_Quality_in_HCBS.pdf

Garavaglia, B. (2007). The confounding influence of age as an explanation for memory loss among older adult long term care. *New Social Worker Online* (Winter). Retrieved from http://www.socialworker.com/home/index2.php?option=com_content&do_pdf=1&id=149

Gelso, C. J., & Hayes, J. A. (1998). The psychotherapy relationship. In *The psychotherapy relationship: Theory, research, and practice* (pp. 22–46). New York: John Wiley & Sons.

Geriatric social work. (n.d.). In M. H. Beers (Ed.-in-Chief) & T. V. Jones (Ed.), *The Merck manual of geriatrics.* Retrieved from http://www.merck.com/mkgr/mmg/sec1/ch9/ch9a.jsp

Germain, C. B., & Gitterman, A. (1986). The life model approach to social work practice revisited. In F. Turner (Ed.), *Social work treatment: Interlocking theoretical approaches* (3rd ed., pp. 618–644). New York: Free Press.

Ginther, S., & Fox, P. (1991). *Alzheimer's Disease Diagnostic and Treatment Center patient data report.* San Francisco: Institute for Health & Aging, University of California, San Francisco.

Greene, R. (1999). *Human behavior theory and social work practice* (2nd ed.) Hawthorne, NY: Aldine Transaction.

Greene, R., Cohen, H., Galambos, C., & Kropf, N. (2007). *Foundations of social work practice in the field of aging: A competency-based approach.* Washington, DC: NASW Press.

Greene, R., & Soniat, B. (1991). Clinical interventions with older adults in need of protection. *Journal of Psychotherapy and the Family, 2,* 1–15.

Grisso, T. (1986). *Evaluating competencies: Forensic assessments and instruments.* New York: Plenum Press.

Grisso, T. (2003) *Evaluating competence* (2nd ed.). New York: Plenum Press.

Harm Reduction Psychotherapy and Training Associates. (n.d.). *What is harm reduction psychotherapy?* Retrieved from http://www.harmreductioncounseling.com/therapy.html

Healy, Tara C. (2003). Ethical decision making: Pressure and uncertainty as complicating factors. *Health & Social Work, 28,* 293–301.

Hooyman, N. R. (2009). *Transforming social work education: The first decade of the Hartford geriatric social work initiative.* New York: John A. Hartford Foundation.

Hooyman, N. R., & Kiyak, H. A. (2005). *Social gerontology: A multidisciplinary perspective* (7th ed.). Boston: Allyn & Bacon.

Institute for Geriatric Social Work. (2005). The shortage of social workers caring for elders and their families. *Social Work, Aging and Public Policy, 1*(1), 1.

Johnson, C. L., & Catalano, D. J. (1981). Childless elderly and their family supports. *Gerontologist, 21,* 610–618.

Jung, C. J. (1969). *The psychology of the transference* (R.C.F. Hull, Trans.). Princeton: Princeton University Press.

Kane, R., & King, C. (Eds.). (1997). *Deciding whether the client can decide: Assessment of decision-making capability.* Minneapolis: University of Minnesota Long-Term Care DECISIONS Resource Center.

Kapp, M. B. (1990). Evaluating decision making capacity in the elderly: A review of the literature. *Journal of Elder Abuse and Neglect, 2*(3/4), 15–24.

Kapp, M. B. (2003). Decisional capacity in theory and practice: Legal process versus "bumbling through." In M. B. Kapp (Ed.), *Ethics, law, and aging review* (Vol. 10, pp. 83–92). New York: Springer.

Kapp, M. B., (2004). Advocacy in an aging society: The varied roles of attorneys. *Generations, 28,* 31–35.

Katz, S. A., Ford, A.B., Moskowitz, R.W., Jackson, B.A., & Jaffe, M. W. (1963). The index of ADL: A standardized measure of biological and psychological function. *JAMA, 185,* 94–101.

Kelly, P. L. (2008, July 1). *Population shifts: Challenges and opportunities for economic and social sustainability.* Paper presented at the Annual Ministerial Review of the Economic and Social Council, United Nations Headquarters, New York.

Kovar, M. G., & Lawton, M. P. (1994). Functional disability: Activities and instrumental activities of daily living. In M. P. Lawton & J. A. Terese (Eds.), *Annual review of gerontology and geriatrics* (Vol. 14, pp. 57–75). New York: Springer.

Krout, J. (1985). Service awareness among the elderly. *Journal of Gerontological Social Work, 9*(1), 7–18.

Lawton, M. P. (1982). Competence, environmental press, and the adaptation of older people. In M. P. Lawton, P. G. Windley, & T. O. Byerts (Eds.), *Aging and the environment: Theoretical approaches* (pp. 33–59). New York: Springer.

Lawton, M. P., & Brody, E. M. (1969). Assessment of older people: Self-maintaining and instrumental activities of daily living. *Gerontologist, 9,* 179–186.

Lawton, M. P., Brody, E. M., & Turner-Massey, P. (1978). The relationships of environmental factors to changes in well-being. *Gerontologist, 18,* 133–137.

Lawton, M. P., & Nahemow, L. (1973). Ecology and the aging process. In C. Eisdorfer & M. P. Lawton (Eds.), *The psychology of adult development and aging* (pp. 619–674). Washington, DC: American Psychological Association.

Lichtenberg, P., MacNeill, S., & Mast, B. (2000). Environmental press and adaptation to disability in hospitalized live-alone older adults. *Gerontologist, 40,* 549–556.

Lipsman, R. (1996). Services and supports to the homebound elderly with mental health needs. *Journal of Long Term Home Health Care, 15*(3), 24–38.

Loewenstein, D. A., & Mogosky, B. (1999). Functional assessment in the older adult patient. In P. Lichtenberg, *Handbook of assessment in clinical gerontology* (pp. 268–281). New York: John Wiley & Sons.

Macdonald, J. G. (2002). The practitioner as researcher. In F. J. Turner (Ed.), *Social work practice: A Canadian perspective* (2nd ed., pp. 492–504). Toronto: Pearson Education Canada.

Marson, D., & Briggs, S. (2001). Assessing competency in Alzheimer's disease: Treatment consent capacity and financial capacity. In S. Gauthier & J. L. Cummings (Eds.), *Alzheimer's disease and related disorders annual: 2001* (pp. 165–192). London: Martin Dunitz.

Marson, D., Earnst, K., Jamil, F., Bartolucci, A., & Harrell, L. (2000). Consistency of physicians' legal standard and personal judgments of competency in patients with Alzheimer's disease. *Journal of American Geriatrics Society, 48,* 911–918.

Marson, D., & Herbert, K. R. (2006). Functional assessment. In D. K. Attix & K. A. Welsh-Bohmer (Eds.), *Geriatric neuropsychology: Assessment and intervention* (pp. 158–197). New York: Guilford Press.

Marson, D., & Ingram, K. (1996). Competency to consent to research: A growing field of research. *Journal of Ethics, Law, and Aging, 2,* 59–63.

Marson, D., McInturff, B., Hawkins, L., Bartolucci, A., & Harrell, L. (1997). Consistency of physicians judgments of capacity to consent in mild Alzheimer's disease. *Journal of the American Geriatrics Society, 45,* 453–457.

Mayhew, M. (2005). Survey of state guardianship laws: Statutory provisions for clinical evaluations. *BIFOCAL, 26,* 1–19.

McCue, M. (1997). The relationship between neuropsychology and functional assessment in the elderly. In P. D. Nussbaum (Ed.), *Handbook of neuropsychology and aging* (pp. 394–408). New York: Plenum Press.

Melady, M. (1992). *Issues in determining competency in the elderly: The role of social work.* Unpublished master's thesis, Catholic University of America.

Miller, W. R. (1983). Motivational interviewing with problem drinkers. *Behavioural Psychotherapy, 11,* 147–172.

Moye, J., Butz, S., Marson, D., Wood, E., and the ABA–APA Assessment of Older Adults Working Group. (2007). A conceptual model and assessment template for capacity evaluation in adult guardianship. *Gerontologist, 47,* 591–603.

Moye, J., Karel, M., Azar, A., & Gurrera, R. (2004). Capacity to consent to treatment: Empirical comparison of three instruments in older adults with and without dementia. *Gerontologist, 44,* 166–175.

Moye, J., & Marson, D. C. (2007). Assessment of decision-making capacity in older adults: An emerging area of practice and research. *Journal of Gerontology, Series B: Psychological Sciences and Social Sciences, 62,* P3–P11.

Moye, J., Wood, S., Edelstein, B., Armesto, J. C., Bower, E. H., Harrison, J. A., & Wood, E. (2007). Clinical evidence in guardianship of older adults is inadequate: Findings from a tri-state study. *Gerontologist, 47,* 604–612.

National Association of Social Workers. (1992). *NASW standards for social work case management.* Retrieved from http://www.socialworkers.org/practice/standards/sw_case_mgmt.asp

National Association of Social Workers. (1999). *Code of ethics.* Washington, DC: Author.

National Association of Social Workers. (2004). *Social work pioneers: Margaret Blenkner (1909–1973).* Retrieved from http://www.naswfoundation.org/pioneers/b/blenkner.htm

National Association of Social Workers. (2005, April 15). *Standards for social work practice in health care settings.* Washington, DC: Author.

National Conference of Commissioners on Uniform State Laws. (1993). *Uniform Health-Care Decisions Act.* Retrieved from http://www.law.upenn.edu/bll/ulc/fnact99/1990s/uhcda93.pdf

Nelson-Becker, H., Chapin, R., & Fast, B. (2009). The strengths model with older adults: Critical practice components. In D. Saleebey (Ed.), *The strengths perspective in social work practice* (5th ed., pp. 148–170). Boston: Allyn & Bacon.

Netting, F. E., Kettner, P. M., & McMurtry, S. L. (2004). *Social work macro practice* (3rd ed). Boston: Pearson Education.

Older Americans Act of 1965, P.L. 89-73, § 79 Stat. 218 (1965).

Pinderhughes, E. (1989). *Understanding race, ethnicity, and power: The key to efficacy in clinical practice.* New York: Free Press.

Rapport. (n.d.). Retrieved from Wikipedia: http://en.wikipedia.org/wiki/Rapport

Ray, M., Bernard, M., & Phillips, J. (2009). *Critical issues in social work with older people.* New York: Palgrave Macmillan.

Roberts-DeGenarro, M. (1987). Developing case management as a practice model. *Social Casework, 68,* 466–470.

Rogers, C. R. (1942). *Counseling and psychotherapy.* Boston: Houghton Mifflin.

Rollnick, S., & Miller, W. R. (1995). What is motivational interviewing? *Behavioural and Cognitive Psychotherapy, 23,* 325–334.

Rothman, J. (1994). *Practice with highly vulnerable clients: Case management and community-based service.* New York: Prentice Hall.

Royall, D. R., Chiodo, L. K., & Polk, M. J. (2000). Correlates of disability among elderly retirees with "subclinical" cognitive impairment. *Journal of Gerontology, Series A: Biological and Medical Sciences, 55,* M541–M546.

Sabatino, C. P. (1996). Competency: Refining our legal fictions. In M. Smyer, K. W. Schaie, & M. B. Kapp (Eds.), *Older adults' decision-making and the law* (pp. 1–28). New York: Springer.

Saleebey, D. (Ed.). (1992). *The strengths perspective in social work practice.* New York: Longman.

Saleebey, D. (Ed.). (2008). *The strengths perspective in social work practice* (5th ed.) Boston: Allyn & Bacon.

Saxena, S., & Maidment, K. (2004). Treatment of compulsive hoarding. *Journal of Clinical Psychology, 60,* 1143–1154.

Schogt, B., & Sadavoy, J. (1987). Assessing the protective service Needs of the impaired elderly living in the community. *Canadian Journal of Psychiatry, 32,* 179–184.

Shanas, E. (1979). Social myth as hypothesis: The case of family relationships of older people. *Gerontologist, 19,* 3–9.

Shipp, K. M., & Branch, L. (1999). The physical environment as a determinant of the health status of older populations. *Canadian Journal on Aging, 18,* 313–327.

Silberfeld, M., & O'Rourke, K. (1994). Cognitive deficits and mental capacity evaluation. *Canadian Journal on Aging, 13,* 539–549.

Smith, R. (2008). *Social work and power.* New York: Palgrave Macmillan.

Smyer, M., Schaie, W. K., & Kapp, M. B. (Eds.). (1996). *Older adults' decision-making and the law.* New York: Springer.

Solomon, B. B. (1976). *Black empowerment: Social work in oppressed communities.* New York: Columbia University Press.

Soniat, B., & Micklos, M. (1993, April). *Working with elderly clients who are resistant to accepting help: A model for clinical assessment and intervention.* Paper presented at the Invitational Preconference of the 14th Annual Meeting of the Southern Gerontological Society, Richmond, VA.

Soniat, B., & Micklos, M. (1994, January). *Working with clients who are resistant to accepting help: Models for assessment and intervention.* Paper presented at the Quarterly Workshop of Howard University & the DC Office on Aging, Washington, DC.

Soniat, B., & Micklos, M. (1995a, June) *Working with clients who are resistant to accepting help: Models for assessment and intervention.* Half-day intensive workshop given at the conference of the American Society on Aging, Washington, DC.

Soniat, B., & Micklos, M. (1995b, November). *Working with clients who are resistant to accepting help: Models for assessment and intervention.* Invitational workshop presentation given at the Maryland Gerontological Society, Baltimore.

Soniat, B., & Micklos, M. (1996). *The capacity–risk model: A guide for assessment and intervention with vulnerable older adults.* Unpublished manuscript.

Soniat, B., & Micklos, M. (1998, October). *Working with clients who are resistant to accepting help: Models for assessment and intervention.* Presentation for the Network of Episcopal Professionals Providing Aging Services, Washington, DC.

Soniat, B., & Micklos, M. (2007, March) *Empowering social workers for community interventions with older adults: A capacity–risk model.* Workshop presentation given at the Annual Conference of the DC Metro Chapter of NASW, Washington, DC.

Soniat, B., & Micklos, M. (2008, June). *Empowering social workers, care managers, and other community based professionals for interventions with vulnerable older adults: A capacity–risk model.* Workshop presentation given to ESM Cares & Sunrise Assisted Living, Washington, DC.

Soniat, B., & Pollack, M. (1992). *Non-traditional support systems of the cognitively impaired older person who lives alone.* Paper presented at the 42nd Annual Program Meeting of the National Council on Aging, Washington, DC.

Soniat, B. A., & Pollack, M. (1993a). Elderly orphans with Alzheimer's disease: The cognitively impaired older person without family. *Clinical Gerontologist, 14,* 33–44.

Soniat, B. A., & Pollack, M. (1993b). Elderly orphans with Alzheimer's disease: Non-traditional support systems. In T. L. Brink (Ed.), *The forgotten aged: Ethnic, psychiatric, and social minorities* (pp. 33–44). New York: Haworth Press.

Soniat, B., & Pollack, M. (1996, May 15). *Elderly orphans: Strengths of non-traditional support systems.* Paper presented at Grand Rounds, George Washington University Medical Center.

Steketee, G., & Frost, R. O. (2007). *Compulsive hoarding and acquiring: Therapist guide.* Oxford: Oxford University Press.

Steketee, G., Frost, R. O., & Kim, H.-J. (2001). Hoarding by elderly people. *Health & Social Work, 26,* 176–184.

Streib, G. F. (1977). Bureaucracies and families: Common themes and directions for further study. In E. Shanas & M. B. Sussman (Eds.), *Family, bureaucracy, and the elderly* (pp. 36–59). Durham NC: Duke University Press.

Tennstedt, S., Harrow, B. S., & Crawford, S. (1996). Informal care vs. formal services: Changes in patterns of care over time. *Journal of Aging and Social Policy, 7,* 71–91.

Therapeutic relationship. (n.d.). Retrieved from Wikipedia: http://en.wikipedia.org/w/index.php?title=Therapeutic_relationship&oldid=301798632

Thursz, D. (1995). Introduction. In D. Thursz, C. Nusberg, & J. Prather (Eds.), *Empowering older people : An international approach* (pp. xi–xiv). Westport, CT: Auburn House.

Tice, C. J., & Perkins, K. (1996). *Mental health issues and aging: Building on the strengths of older persons.* Pacific Grove, CA: Brooks/Cole.

Tobin, D. (2007, Spring). New England Housing Consortium update. *New England Hoarding Consortium Newsletter.* Retrieved from http://www.science.smith.edu/departments/PSYCH/rfrost/NEHC_Newsletter_April_2007.pdf

Transference. (n.d.). Retrieved from Wikipedia: http://en.wikipedia.org/wiki/Transference

Uniform Guardianship and Protective Proceedings Act (UGPPA). (1997). Retrieved from http://www.law.upenn.edu/bll/archives/ucl/ugppa/ugppa97.htm

United Nations. (2007). *World population aging.* Geneva: UN Department of Economic and Social Affairs, Population Division.

U.S. Department of Health and Human Services, Administration on Aging. (2008). *A profile of older Americans: 2008.* Retrieved from http://www.aoa.gov/AoARoot/Aging_Statistics/Profile/index.aspx

Virginia State Board of Social Services. (2001). *Adult protective services minimum training standards.* Retrieved from the Virginia Department of Social Services Web site: http://www.dss.virginia.gov/family/as/aps.cgi

Wan, H., Sengupta, M., Velkoff, V. A., & DeBarros, K. A. (2005). *U.S. Census Bureau, current publication reports, 65 + in the United States: 2005.* Washington, DC: U.S. Government Printing Office.

Webber P. A., Fox, P., & Burnette, D. (1994). Living alone with Alzheimer's disease: Effects on health and social service utilization patterns. *Gerontologist, 34,* 8–14.

Whitaker, T., Weismiller, T., & Clark, E. (2006). *Landmark study warns of impending labor force shortages for social work profession.* Retrieved from http://www.socialworkers.org/press room/2006/030806.asp

Wiener, J., Hanley, R., Clark, R., & Van Nostrand, J. (1990). Measuring the activities of daily living: Comparisons across national surveys. *Journal of Gerontology, 45,* S229–S237.

Willis, S. L. (1996). Assessing everyday competence in the cognitively challenged elderly. In M. Smyer, W. K. Schaie, & M. B. Kapp (Eds.), *Older adults' decision-making and the law* (pp. 87–127). New York: Springer.

Wolff, K. R. (1990). Determining patient competency in treatment refusal cases. *Georgia Law Review, 24,* 733–743.

Wolinsky, F. D., Callahan, C. M., Fitzgerald, J. F., & Johnson, R. J. (1993). Changes in functional status and the risks of subsequent nursing home placement and death. *Journal of Gerontology: Social Sciences, 48,* S94–S101.

Worobey, J. L., & Angel, R. J. (1990). Functional capacity and living arrangements of unmarried elderly persons. *Journal of Gerontology, 45,* S95–S101.

Yagoda, L. (2004, May). *Case management with older adults: A social work perspective.* Retrieved from http://www.socialworkers.org/practice/aging/aging0504.pdf

Zarit, S., & Zarit, J. M. (2007) *Mental disorders in older adults: Fundamentals of assessment and treatment* (2nd. ed.).New York: Guilford Press.

Index